I'M UNDER THE WATCHFUL EYES OF GOD

I'M UNDER THE WATCHFUL EYES OF GOD

NADIA AWWAD

To order additional copies of this book, contact:
Xlibris
1-888-795-4274
www.Xlibris.com
Orders@Xlibris.com
788122

CONTENTS

Chapter 1   Born in the Wilderness 1

Chapter 2   Labeled and Rejected 11

Chapter 3   911 Emergency...19

Chapter 4   Seasons Change..27

Chapter 5   Young Disciple in Formation................................33

Chapter 6   Faith Over Fear 37

Chapter 7   Broken Vessel 45

Chapter 8   Worthy..53

Chapter 9   Burned out but Blessed..57

Chapter 10 Turning Point..61

Chapter 11 Jesus is Alive..69

Chapter 12 Resurrection Power 73

Chapter 13 Unshakable 79

Chapter 14 Steady Building...85

Chapter 15 Life as A Disciple...93

Chapter 16 Holy Land Experience 99

Book summary

Growing up, Author Nadia Awwad received compliments on her looks and her slim figure and began modeling professionally at age 15. Like many, she struggled with an identity crisis. Her ambition was to be a supermodel, but after an encounter with Jesus Christ she found that she was "God's model." Later she discovered that the world brought her outward happiness, but Jesus filled her soul with joy. Struggling between the world and the Word, her decision would change her life. Would she follow her will or Jesus' will for her life? Eventually, she forsook everything and ran to God for his divine purpose. She tells a story of great devotion to ministry, followed by crisis after crisis, which left her with a broken heart. Never losing hope in the Word, she conquered every difficult trial, inspiring people to be overcomers. That means trusting Jesus while going through storms in life.

CHAPTER 1

Born in the Wilderness

I came in with a loud bang. Fireworks blast off as I am born January 1 at 12:10 AM. This is a time for celebration. I am born. But I had a surprise as life would sneak a curve in now and then. Later, my mother sarcastically said, "You were born too late for me to receive a tax credit that year." Growing up my mom always had a wonderful sense of humor and was always positive and uplifting. She could always find the good in each person and every situation. God knew what He was doing, for I never think of being born at the wrong time no matter what. Who can choose when they are born? The choosing would come later as I trusted God more. I am just getting started on this journey.

My earliest childhood memories were of being shy and reserved. At the age of the three my mom would sit me on the couch to watch Sesame Street and I will literally sit there all day; no movement: no crying in such a soft peaceful, easy, gentle spirit. My mother said I was the best baby; I was low maintenance child because I would not cry. I sat so still my sisters would make jokes as they pinched me to see if I was asleep or not. I never cried, but I whined a few times. I am thinking of better days to come. The test is just starting, and I am in the wilderness.

From a young age, I operated in the gifting of the seer anointing. I would have vivid dreams of my family members and sharp discernment of people's motives at heart. There were times when I shared my dreams with my mother when I explained an event that would happen to her, and later she found it to be true. She was shocked but quietly kept the matter to herself. Still today, my mom tells everyone I was a Heaven sent a baby, and that God had his hand on me.

Since my early years, my interest was in science. Instead of playing with the other kids at recess, I would stay at my teacher's desk asking questions. When the children saw me staying in the classroom, they labeled me as the teacher's pet. Yet, all I was doing was seeking knowledge and understanding. Growing up, I was a curious kid and shy. I was always asking questions and searching for wisdom and knowledge about everything. Older people naturally drew me into conversations. I could communicate well with my teacher, and I enjoy being alone reading books, instead of playing with the children. Some might say I was an outcast, with the other kids calling me names and teasing me because I was tall and skinny. My classmates would say harmful jokes and I would run away from all the teasing and confusion. I didn't want to defend myself, nor tell my teacher. So, I overlooked all the insults and kept quiet. Yet, deep inside I was sad because I didn't fit in with the other children. I just wanted the kids to show love and acceptance towards me.

As I matured, my slim build became an asset, and during my adolescent years, everywhere I went people assumed I was a model. I took the constant stream of compliments to heart and started modeling professionally at age 15. I studied fashion trends and register for acting classes. Soon after this, I appeared in several television commercials, one for PBS and one promoting Houston Community College, where I then became the school's branding model for their magazines and marketing materials. Several months later, I accepted another opportunity to become the cover model for JMZ Magazine and did more commercials starting with Doritos. As the words of others glorified my physical image in print and video, my fame rose fast and my fortune increased. At that time, I thought that I was living the best life. I was happy living a very glamorous life, loving all forms of art and fashion-- who wouldn't feel good about that? Later, I realized it was never about modeling my glory, but it was about drawing other people to God's glory within me and revealing their inner light! Ultimately, worldly desires and success continued to rise, yet I was left with a sense of worthlessness and lack of identity. "For what shall it profit a man, if he shall gain the whole world, and lose his own soul?" (Mark 8:36 KJV)) What I didn't know at the time was that I was trying to control my destiny, and would later learn to allow the Holy Spirit to direct me. The ways of the world brought me outward happiness, but I later found inward joy in Christ Jesus.

When I was in the entertainment industry I was making good money, but I was unaware of my spiritual life at that time. I enjoyed the glamorous life of being on television and meeting celebrities, and the best part was the residual income. From a young age, I wasn't interested in following any religion, and my ambition was to achieve my own goals. Therefore, I disciplined myself and avoided any distractions that would hinder me from achieving my goals and attaining success. Independent from an early age, I was used to doing things for myself, but I had to depend on God to care for me; his provision and his instruction for my life. I had very early success, yet I still felt there was something missing, but I couldn't describe what it was. You might say it was an "existential crisis." I had accumulated great riches, and accomplish a lot of my goals, but I was still searching to find myself. Eventually, I would discover that there is a living God that I was missing out on. Before I accepted Jesus Christ as my Lord and Savior, I was living a life without purpose or meaning.

I must admit, I was a nerd in college. I graduated with honors and receive five rewards on the Dean's list at the University of Houston-Downtown, with a Bachelor's Degree in Business Marketing. Driven, enthusiastic, and successful life was going well for me in the entertainment industry. Yet, there was still something missing; I needed to fill an emptiness—a hole inside, that I found out later was a "God-shaped hole." At that time, I did not understand God. I never knew the indescribable breadth and depth of God's love.

Based on my experiences, I thought that life was all about graduating with honors, working on a lucrative job, and becoming prosperous in life. This is true to an extent; but it's important for people to discover their gifts and identity in Christ Jesus, then we can fulfil our purpose effortlessly. Its was easy to build life on my profession and success, but I still missed the most important thing, which was the revelation that I am the beloved of God. Like many of us, especially in our unsaved youth, I was living rather superficially. Focusing on the limelight, the glamorous life and status quo, I did what made others happy, instead of listening to my inner voice.

Constantly living to be accepted by others, yet I never knew that I am fully accepted in God. Spending so much effort trying to make people understand me, I would sometimes jeopardize my happiness and freedom. It's good to display selfless love: which means putting others needs and desires before you; but there must be a balance. Eventually, I had to set up boundaries for people and learn how to stand boldly and say "NO", while still feeling confident in my decision. Often, inharmonious relationships made me nervous; I could not stand for people to be mad at me. I would always want to fix problems because I cared and didn't want to offend anyone. All I could do was continue to speak love and truth, learning that it doesn't matter what other people think of me. Overextending myself to people had finally come to an end. I passed the test and continued to do good deeds as much as possible and allowed goodness to follow me. Finally, I had an experience that changed my life forever.

Say yes to that little inclination, because you don't know what the next "Yes" will be. A simple visit to the post office led me to the biggest "Yes" of my life. That day, I went to the post office and I ran across a handicap lady. I greeted her and ask her if I could help her carry her bags to her car. That very moment, she smiled and handed me a flyer and invited me to go to church with her. Then, she thanked me for my kindness and walked away. It puzzled me, but I listened to my intuition and kept the flyer. I thought to myself, perhaps, everything happens for a reason. So, I went to church the next day. Attending the church for the first time wasn't too bad. It was entertaining to hear the preacher dance and shout the Word of God. The sermon topic was the "Power of Prayer." I didn't have a great understanding of walking in faith or praying to apply the scriptures. After the sermon, I learned some precious information. During the end of the service, the preacher asked for people to come up that want a touch from God. At first, I hesitated, then I boldly went up to the altar. At that moment, I heard the preacher prophesy information about my life. The prophetic word given was about my family and childhood experiences, as well as information about God calling me as a Prophetess to the nation. That very day, I was told that in the future I would be performing healing, prophecies, and sermons. The information was accurate about my family, but I wasn't confident about the prospect of operating in the office of a Prophetess. Puzzled and amazed, I stood there speechless. As I was walking back to my seat, the usher handed me a welcome package and a small pocket bible. A kept the bible, but I didn't begin to study it. After that day, I ponder the Christian faith. Yet, I still wasn't convinced to join the church organization.

I can recall a time in my life when I experienced painful consecutive cramps that was on and off for three years. The pain literally brought me to my knees until I saw a doctor who told me "You have to have surgery. There's a great chance you'll never have children." Initially, I thought I would have to face this illness alone and have to take the chance of never having children if I do this surgery. What a tough decision to make? Feeling desperate, I immediately cried out to God with all my heart and soul. My situation reminds me of what Hannah experience when she made a vow to say, "Lord Almighty, if you will only look on your servant's misery and remember me, and not forget your servant." (1 Samuel 1:11) My situation was similar, I strike a bargain with God to heal me and I promise to devote my life as a living sacrifice to him. Be careful what you ask for, God may take you up on it! Just as Abraham bargain with God to have mercy on Lot and spare the righteous people in Sodom and Gomorrah. I took the same approach, and later God took me up on my promise. Although we are not in a position to barter with God, He may still answer a prayer that is aligned with the Holy Word.

I constantly prayed for divine healing of an ovarian cyst that had invaded my body. I felt that there was hope for me, so I walked in radical faith. Being a child of God, a child of the Light, I refused to accept the medical opinion on my body. Growing into a Prayer Warrior and Healer, I prayed and prayed for wholeness and health. Within a month, there was no sign of disease—a disease that God had rebuked. Upon reading the new results, the doctor was so surprised, her mouth fell open with shock. She told me, to my delight, that I actually could have children. My healing was so complete; it was like I'd never been sick. Swelling in the ovarian cyst which had caused the cramps had not only gone down, but it had completely disappeared! I told the Divine One, "God, there is so much power in your word. For it is written, "No word from God will ever fail." (Luke 1:37 NIV). The word comforted me and gave me hope in God's promises. I will serve you forever my Lord King.

My supernatural healing brought me to experience Jesus Christ's dunamis power, however, I still had to learn more about him. During intimate worship in my home, the Holy Spirit came upon me in my "sacred room" (a room set-aside for worship and prayer). I remember feeling a hot fire in my heart, a tingling sensation in my hands, and I began speaking in tongues of fire. So this was the same experience that happened to the Pentecostal church in Acts, chapter two. "When the day of Pentecost came, they were all together in one place. Suddenly a sound like the blowing of a violent wind came from heaven and filled the whole house where they were sitting. They saw what seemed to be tongues of fire that separated and came to rest on each of them. They filled were all filled by the Holy Spirit and spoke in other tongues as the Spirit enabled them." (Acts 2:1-4 NIV).

I experienced the baptism of the Holy Spirit, speaking in new tongues as the evidence. What I encountered after my healing, was a wonderful, indescribable feeling; I felt so close to God that I felt his breath under my nose and movement under my skin. Amazing grace, God captured my heart and filled me with the fullness of his spirit. I'm sure you're thinking, what are tongues of fire? Tongues symbolize speech and the communication of the gospel. Fire symbolizes the power and presence of God (Hebrews 12:29) which burns and purifies undesirable elements in our lives. The Holy Spirit set our hearts aflame to ignite the lives of others. God captured my heart and filled me with the fullness of his spirit. Finding Christ was my greatest treasure because I found my identity in him and it has made me complete through the unity of his Holy Spirit. (Colossians 2:10) Surrendering my life fully, now I was a new person, equipped for life and satisfied in God.

The Lord confirmed the prophecy that the preacher spoke over my life and revealed his plans for me. I was to prepare myself to lead a nation by spreading the Hope of Glory and by sharing my testimony of God's goodness. Everyday, I was walking from glory to glory, and my life had been a walking miracle.

After my conversion, Jesus drew my heart toward studying John 10:30, where Jesus says, " I and the Father are one." Jesus and his Father are not the same person, but they are one in essence and nature. Jesus is not a mere teacher, but he is God living in flesh (also known as the living Word), and the Holy Spirit is the pure living spirit in our Heavenly Father.

The Holy Spirit is not an energy, but He is a person. Scriptures to support the personhood of the Holy Spirit are many. For example it's possible to grieve the Holy Spirit (Ephesians 4:30), Spirit can be sinned against, (Isaiah 63:10) and lied to. (Acts 5:3) We are to obey him (Act 10:19-21) and honor him (Psalm 51:11). The Holy Spirit's work is to draw you near to him, convict your conscious of sin, and enlighten you with understanding. Also, he grants repentance; sanctifies, fills, empowers, guides, comforts, and counsels. Apart from the Holy Spirit, we can do nothing. The precious Holy Spirit is believers' best friend, helper, and advocate that Jesus promised us. (Luke 24:49)

All together, there is the Three Godhead (Trinity), which is the Father, Son, and Holy Spirit- three persons in one God. Being created in the likeness of God, human beings share our own three parts in one, which is the Body, Soul, Spirit. Everything is connected together and working in unity. There is only One God with three parts that are in sync and equally working together. These names of God will be used interchangeably, always referring to the one God: Father, Jesus-the Son of God, and the Precious Holy Spirit.

Spending time in the glory realm, I felt a deep peace and closeness with God. My healing opened my eyes to the fact I had been living out of my power and needed to live under God's power. As I matured in the Word of God, I became a conduit for God's light and love, shining an inner light onto the darkness of others' sickness and "dis-ease," confidently knowing that darkness is no match for the light, and I was a walking miracle. However, I still had to go through the sanctification process to mature in character and grow spiritually. My healing played a great role in my conversion, it was the grace of God that implanted his Holy Spirit in my heart and gave me the new power to live for him. Immediately, I told God, "Show me your Divine Light that I may share it with others." God was faithful to answer my prayers.

When I was living without God's revelation I was a victim of my circumstances. I would speak my victimhood and my ailments into existence. "I don't have this or that," I would say. "I'm sick… I don't have enough money…I'll never gets better." When I changed my words, I changed my reality. In the physical realm, we use words to communicate. In the spiritual realm, we use words to manifest healing and power. "Let the weak say I am strong". (Joel 3:10 KJV) Now I am strong in this world because God tells me that in Him I am strong. I'm no longer at the mercy of my circumstances. "This is my comfort and consolation in my affliction: that your word has revived me and given me life" (Psalm 119:50 KJV). God allows our weakness to draw us to him. He becomes our strength when we remain in him and his word remains in us.

Reminiscing on my past illness, sometimes I would clutter my mind with negative thoughts, but when I aligned my words with God's words; everything changed in my life for the best! This is my secret of how I healed anxiety attacks. If you are having problems being positive, meditate on the affirmation listed below daily. This will renew your mind in the Word of God. Faith comes by hearing and hearing by the Word of God. (Roman 10:17)

I can do all things through Christ, who strengthens me (Phi. 4:13)
I am the righteousness of God in Christ (2 Cor. 5:21)
I am the head and not the tail (Deut. 28:13)
I am sitting in heavenly places in Christ (Eph. 2:6)
I am victoriously winning all of my battles (Roman 8:37)
I am in a position to be a blessing (Deuteronomy 28:12)
I am overflowing with wealth (2 Corinthians 8:9)
I am confident that God hears me (1 John 5:14)
I am capable of reversing the attacks of Satan (Deuteronomy 28:7)
I am created in the image of God. (Genesis 1:27)
I am blessed when I come in and blessed when I go out (Deuteronomy 28:6)
I am confident that He who has begun a good work in me will complete it until the day of Jesus Christ (Philippians 1:6).

In the next chapter, I will explain more in detail my challenges and intimate relationship with Christ Jesus. I've experienced a great time with Jesus, as well as painful moments. Through all circumstances, I am under the Watchful eyes of God. I am well acquainted with long-suffering, one of the fruits of the spirit. (Galatians 5:22-23) Many of you reading this book will discover the beauty and ashes of my journey with Christ Jesus. Perhaps, some of you reading the book will be inspired and find the courage to overcome any challenges in life. Even when you hit rock bottom, there is always hope. As long as you keep your eyes fixed on Jesus Christ, you will discover your inner strength, power, and greatest treasure within. Walking with God gives one the confidence, protection, and peace to overcome any difficulty. I am honored to share my experiences with you, hopefully, you can use the information provided to better understand the positive effect of the long-suffering and storms of life. God uses good and bad circumstances for his good and glory.There nothing we can hide from God sight or out of his control. In fact, he knows what we will pray before a word comes out of our mouth. This book was born out of experience, pain, and wisdom. The first chapters explain my life story, the middle section is life trials, and lastly the blessing that comes from continually trusting in God despite your circumstances. I pray that the Lord would open your eyes of understanding the treasures God gives us in the deepest and darkest moments in our lives. In Jesus name. Amen.

CHAPTER 2

Labeled and Rejected

Living the new life as a Christian was difficult. Daily, I had to crucify my desires and daily renew my mind in the Holy Scriptures. Every day, I strived to walk upright and pleasing life toward the Lord. Jesus makes us holy and righteous when we fully daily surrender to the leading of the Holy Spirit and trust in his word. The sanctifying process had begun. As I grew in the knowledge of Christ Jesus, I had to change my lifestyle.

All praise to the Lord! The Lord showed me I must prepare myself for the ministry by daily inwardly sanctifying myself by consistently renewing my mind, studying scriptures, and applying the word to my life. The biblical law convicted me of flawed thinking and the Holy Spirit renewed, reeducated, counseled, and redirected my mind to the mind of Christ Jesus. It is vital that Christians seek God first because the Bible is our only roadmap to success. Daily, I set goals and discipline myself for the spiritual journey that was ahead of me. Nothing good comes easy, think about an athlete experiencing pain during training. I had to sacrifice time, personal life, sleep, stability, and entertainment to focus on fulfilling God's purpose for my life. My strict schedule was comprised of daily bible study, worship, prayer, and fellowship with other Christians. As I mentioned in Chapter one, after the supernatural healing from God, I vowed to serve him forever.

When I fed on what the world offered me, I felt loved, adored, and accepted. However, when I preached the word, I experienced rejection and was judged by people. It seems as if spreading the Word and traveling the world were signs of my arrogance. During this struggle between the world's calling and the Word's calling, I got offers to take modeling or advertising jobs. Yet, I no longer felt comfortable doing some movie character roles, but when I passed on business offers; they accused me of being "Holier than Thou." The world reminded me that if I didn't follow the rules of the world, I had nothing, "but according to Christ," I knew for certain, "I'd found everything."

I experienced extreme trials with my talent agencies. It was a more physical temptation for me to do what came easily at that moment or obey God. "The tempter came to him and said, 'If you are the Son of God, tell these stones to become bread.' Jesus answered, 'It is written, 'Man shall not live on bread alone, but on every word that comes from the mouth of God'" (Matthew 4:3-4 NIV). There is power in the Word. Ever since Jesus Christ has come into my life, I have never been the same. I no longer lived my life based on worldly pursuits or selfish ambition. My life was centered on my beautiful Savior and my desires changed. All human ambition is self-referential and self reliant, but spiritual ambition is when the Lord is guiding your steps based on his purpose. I decided to submit to my Lord "Thy will be done, not mine." (Matthew 6:10 KJV) It's by faith, work, and the grace of God that we achieve success effortlessly. The word of God was consistently in my heart and influencing my daily decisions and reminded me how to live a holy and righteous life.

I signed my first contract with one of the biggest modeling agencies in the world, which led to visiting New York City. I was booked for a high-paying job, which presented the greatest temptation of my life, when I was offered an opportunity to be in a national cigarette campaign as a model and actress for a major commercial. This project would pay a large amount of money including residual income per commercial airing. I had every reason to go back to the world with mouthwatering offers from my talent agency and other business opportunities. With no hesitation, I decline on the offer because I refuse to do anything that would bring dishonor to Christ Jesus. Perhaps, the devil is tempting my faithfulness to Jesus, I give up my desires of becoming a supermodel and submit to God's plan for my life.

No compromising with sin for popularity or money. As I can recall from the scriptures, the devil offers the entire world to Jesus if he would bow down and worship him" If you bow down and worship me, he said, 'I will give you all this.' Jesus said to him, 'Get away from me, Satan! It is written, 'Worship the Lord your God. He is the only one you should serve.'" (Matthew 4:9-10 NIV) Today, the devil offers us the world by trying to entice us with materialism and power. I resisted the temptation by allowing the word of God to be my only influence. Satan was trying to distort my perception by making the focus on materialism, fame, and power. Jesus says it best in Matthew 6:24 NIV, "No one can serve two masters. Either you will hate the one and love the other, or you will be devoted to the one and despise the other. You cannot serve both God and money." Often we live in a materialistic society where many people serve money or even makes it an idol. Some people spend all their lives chasing money and believe that what it can buy outweighs their commitment to God and spiritual matters. Whatever you give attention to has power over you, Can you honestly say that God or money is your master? One way to know the answer to this question is by observing your thoughts during meditation. What occupies your mind? It is your thoughts, time, and effort in life that has mastery over your life.

In my situation, The Lord has called me to preach the gospel undiluted, no turning back to worldly jobs for fame, influence or money. I had to give up material pursuits: the love I have for Jesus supersedes all things. Love not money or cars, men or earthly possession compared to the kingdom of God. For it is written, "Keep your lives free from the love of money and be content with what you have, because God has said, " Never will I leave; never will I forsake you." (Hebrews 13:5 NIV)

My true value is the word of God, not money. Jesus is infinitely more valuable than anything I could ever possess in this world. Some people believe that prosperity and success come from having power, influential personal contacts, or a relentless desire to get ahead. Yet this is not true, all blessing comes from our Heavenly Father. We never have to lower our Christian standards to be successful. It only requires a small task to walk in the divine favor, abundance, and blessing of God: which is to study, meditate, and obey the guidance of the Holy Spirit. (Deuteronomy 8:18) All prosperity comes from allowing Godly solutions. As I drew closer to the Father's heart, I discovered that the Lord's purpose for his children is for us to enjoy our gifts that we have and use them for his glory; it is not about what we accumulate on earth, but it's about becoming a blessing to others while using our gifts.

As a result of declining the huge cigarette campaign, my booking agency removed me from their website, which resulted in a huge financial loss for me. Often I faced criticism from my industry friends. I no longer received large volumes of casting jobs; the next day I had a meeting with the president of the agency and she decided to modify my contract. Consequently, I was unable to audition directly with potential clients and I lost job opportunities. That treatment from a former ally felt terrible, so I terminated my contract and moved on.

Even though my Christian faith caused me to experience persecution, I wasn't going to let that discourage me from fulfilling my dreams. As I continue to walk with Jesus and share my faith, people constantly label me. Labeling is when others define someone based on the perspective they have on that person, whether or not it's true. I am more than a label, and I learned how to overcome other people's judgments about me by the Word. God has given me a new name (Isaiah 62:2), a new purpose (Luke 5:10) and a new future (Jeremiah. 29:11). I am no longer the model of the world; I am whatever God says about me. I overcame the guilt from my past failures and shame that came from people mocking me, and I had the courage to start over and rebuild my new life with my Lord. For it is written, "There is no condemnation for those who are in Christ Jesus" (Roman 8:1 KJV). The world may judge me negatively for my deeds, but being true to myself is better than being a liar just to impress everyone. I learned that sometimes God will allow people to reject me to protect me, but in all things what matters is that Jesus' name would be magnified during my sufferings. No matter who tries to sabotage me, Jesus commands my destiny. For it is written, "No weapon formed against you shall prosper, and every tongue that rises against me shall be condemned" (Isaiah 54:17 KJV). Regardless of my circumstances, I have the confidence to believe that God has not forgotten about me. God has a plan for my life, and I have determined me to fulfill my destiny.

Refusing to compromise my faith and speaking the Word boldly caused my old friends to reject me. It was a painful experience. It almost destroyed my self-esteem by getting me to believe in Satan's lies, which could happen to anybody if you don't feel good enough. Some people disrespected and didn't appreciate my sacrifice of service, however, I never change my love towards them. Prior to my healing from rejection, I began to socially withdraw from everyone; I continued to lick my wounds from the pain of rejection. Satan's goal is to get believers to reject the love of God. Without love, faith will not work. (Galatians 5: 6, a faith which worketh by love). Faith expresses itself through genuine love and love manifest itself in giving. "For God so loved the world, that he gave his only begotten Son, that whosoever believeth in him should not perish, but have everlasting life." (John 3:16 KJV) The greatest act of love is sacrificial giving with no thought of receiving anything in return. Without genuine love, we will not have great faith. Love is the essence of life and the very nature of our Lord. I am the beloved of God, perhaps that's the reason the devil continues to oppose me.

This was a point in my life when the devil harasses and challenged my identity in Christ Jesus. The way I fought back false accusation was through the name of God which is "I am who I am"- (Exodus 3:14 KJV) The name I AM shows God's unchanging character: God is the same yesterday, today, and forever. (Hebrews 13:8) Although I knew who I was in Christ, with so much outside pressure from others, at times, I began to second-guess myself. What or who defines who you are? Is it your career? Is it what your parents think of you? Is it what your friends think of you? Is it how much money you have? Is it how physically fit, or tall you are? When passing away, what would define who you are in life? The simple answer is; I am whatever God says I am. I hold strong on my confession and stand up boldly to speak the word of God over my life. I AM God Model! Our world is framed based on words spoken, therefore; believers must make a habit to decree positive affirmation while using the power name of God, which is "I Am" by faith to manifest words into reality.

Whenever someone bases their identity on a career or something other than what God's Word says, they make themselves vulnerable to the damage of rejection. I never based my identity on what my parents, teachers, or friends thought of me. I refused to let the devil deceive the world about who I am, I boldly stood up and commanded over my life every promises concerning my life. My identity and direction are built around the testimony of Jesus; not the accusation. We have defeated Satan through the power of the Cross. As a born-again Christian, we can be attacked or afflicted but it will never destroy us. I believe that God brings suffering into my life for others' sake. Suffering strengthens and allows me to comfort others who are weak. (2 Corinthians 1:3-11) Physical strength is measured by what we can carry; spiritual strengths come by what we can bear. I'm not ashamed of sharing my vulnerabilities, it was never about me, but it's all about Jesus Christ being glorified in my weaknesses. (2 Corinthians 12:9)

Favor is not fair, and the price to pay is rejection. I needed to change my perspective on how others viewed me, gave up trying to control what other people thought, and moved on with my own life. Nothing would stop me from fulfilling my dreams, I only needed God approval. This reminds me of Caleb in Numbers 14 NIV, ("But because my servant Caleb has a different spirit and follows me wholeheartedly, I will bring him into the land he went to, and his descendants will inherit it"); who believed God reported about his life, I, too, am righteous of Christ Jesus, I am fearfully and wonderfully made, I am healed, I am blessed, I am strong, I am what God says I am. Just as Caleb faced giants, I faced the "giants" of rejection and I was able to overcome by the revelation of the word of God. In life, we only rise as high as our declaration: "So as a man thinks, so is he." (Proverbs 23:7NIV)

There is a huge price to pay to identify with Christ Jesus. As I mentioned earlier, walking away from modeling opportunities, was a big sacrifice; I lost not only business opportunities but dear friendships. However, after I received salvation, people's attitudes changed about me. My old entertainment industry friends didn't like my new lifestyle of walking in holiness, and it was time for me to let go of those unequally yoked relationships. For it is written, "Do not be yoked together with unbelievers. For what do righteousness and wickedness have in common? Or what fellowship can light have with darkness?" (2 Corinthians 6:14 NIV) This does not mean that, as believers, we should isolate ourselves from non-believers, but that we should not allow anyone to get in the way of our walk with Jesus. We must be careful to guard the treasure that we have been graced with.

Giving up a relationship, job, or habit that is against God's will may seem just as painful as cutting off a hand, but Christ is worth any possible loss or discomfort. Nothing should stand in the way of faith. It wasn't because I thought I was better; it was because I have to protect the prophetic assignment on my life. It didn't happen right away; I was struggling between two minds. I wanted to keep these people close and to heal them with love, but they weren't good for me. Change isn't always easy, yet I will walk away from everything familiar including my desire of becoming a fashion model. The moment that I was converted to Christianity, I learned that I wasn't the world's fashion model, but we base my identity upon the Word of God, and what God has to say about me. I am the mouthpiece of God, not a worldly supermodel. Christ Jesus is the unshakable rock I build my worth upon. (Matthew 16:18)

Put the devil to shame, I know who I am. God's Word tells us that without being rooted and grounded in the love and acceptance of God, we can never experience the fullness of God in our lives: And to know the love of Christ, which passeth knowledge, that ye might be filled with all the fullness of God. (Ephesians 3:19) Christian receive the fullness of God through faith in the word, prayer, and daily living for him. Ultimately, all humans share the same purpose which is to love everyone and bring glory to our Heavenly Father. God alone is the creator and sustainer of everything, we reflect Jesus Christ—which is love. God wants humans to reflect love, to be accepted and appreciated. It was time for me to move on to the next chapter in my life.

CHAPTER 3

---

911 Emergency

Having moved on to a new modeling agency, I was making good money and life for me was going well. But due to a decrease in the print industry, I was forced to supplement my income by working at a marketing firm. While working in the office, I received a call from my landlord that my apartment was on fire. My dog died because of smoke inhalation. My heart was heavy to witness my dog die. Fifteen minutes later, the veterinarian had her cremated. I found that my perfect life wasn't so perfect, yet I still praised God for protecting my life from this massive apartment fire. It's never fun to start over completely in life, but I knew that God would faithfully get me through this tough season. The next day, I received a call from my job saying that, due to the economic crisis, my contract was terminated. Now, I was without an apartment and had no job, and my business investments weren't going too well. "There is still hope," I constantly told myself. I did not understand what my next move would be. I cried out to God, "Lord order my steps. Where do I go from here? A part of me felt that it shatters my life and another other part felt that God is preparing better things for me. I'm stuck between a rock and a hard place. After wrestling with my thoughts for a half an hour, I felt led in the spirit to drive to my prayer mountain for divine direction. I sorely needed time to regroup.

When faced with a big crisis, I pull away from people and go out into nature to reconnect with the Holy Spirit. Any natural place will do, but I have a special location where I feel most connected spiritually with my Jesus. I desperately needed to hear a word from God, without distraction. Continually, throughout the scriptures, we notice Jesus taking time for solitude and silent moments in the gospels. Spending time with God in prayer nurtures a vital relationship and equips me to meet life's challenges and struggles. I didn't run to God only during hard times, but I disciplined myself to consistently spend time in the Word of God, which would help me grow spiritually and see things from God's perspective. Mark 1:35 is a perfect example of Jesus withdrawing from people for prayer, "Very early in the morning, while it was still dark, Jesus got up, left the house and went off to a solitary place, where he prayed" (Mark 1:35 NIV). Often it is easy to get distracted and busy with life's responsibilities, however, we must never neglect times of fellowship, worship, and prayer.

I drove to my prayer mountain, almost a two-hour drive to the Hill Country, to a campsite and prayed all day, and slept in the car when it got dark outside. I thought to myself, "Holy Spirit move me to where I belong." Things were difficult, but I didn't give up my hope in God. I fasted and prayed. I didn't allow this situation to make me give up on God, instead, I pushed closer. Even through delays, limitations, and hardships cause me to shed a lot of tears, I believed that the Lord will provide, all I can do is be patient, seek God, work hard, and trust that everything is working for my good. It wasn't easy. Often, I was torn between the two wills: God's will for my life or my own willfulness. I knew that God wanted me to live by faith, not by sight. I kept my eyes fixed on Jesus Christ, as the basis for my security. My only option was to submit to God's authority and rest in his care.

The moment I accepted the pain and pleasure of serving God, it was all about putting the pursuit of God's presence and wisdom above all things. Then, I was following Jesus and I knew what it would take to live abundantly. Even though it may have looked like the problem surrounded me, I knew that the Lord was still by my side. I was thankful that I was still alive; I continually encouraged myself by contemplating the goodness of the Lord. As I sat on my "holy rock," I reminisced on the memories of God's miracles and faithfulness that sustained my life through difficulties. I knew that God was capable and trustworthy to restore me. God is my only true security, strength, and hope; I have Jesus and that is enough for me. I continued to pray for God to give me the supernatural strength for this trial and give me a clearer perspective on what is happening in my life. Regardless of the reason for this huge loss, I kept my vow to serve God forever. No matter the reason for our suffering, Jesus has the power to help us deal with it. Never lose hope.

During this huge loss, I was lacking nothing. God provided all of my needs (Philippian 4:19). Trusting God despite our negative circumstances honors him. Based on my experience, I can testify that whatever we need on the earth, "Jehovah-Jireh is our provider." Similar to the Abraham story, God was faithful to provide for me in miraculous ways. (Genesis 22:8). By placing our confidence in Christ, our attitudes change from wanting everything to accepting his provision and power to live for him. "The Lord is my shepherd; I shall not want." (Psalms 23:1 KJV) Have you ever been in a hopeless situation? When facing difficult trials, I want to encourage you to recall how good God has been in the past. Showing gratitude toward God's past victories will strengthen your faith to continue to walk righteously. The Lord wants us to be good stewards of our money, however we should never put our trust and security in material possessions. Prosperity is a mindset, so I spoke abundance over my lack, even during the most tragic events in my life.

After hard work and prayer, three months later, God blessed me with a new home, yet I still had challenges to face. For a very short period of time, I lived out of my car, camping on the prayer mountain, constantly seeking the face of God. When I left the campsite, my face had a different glow, well at least that's what everyone told me. I definitely was not the same person who entered it. I found out more about my true self and deep revelations. There were things I need to change in me; they just won't be changed by feeling bad about myself or trying hard to fix them. That isn't how wholeness works. During my journey of deep discovery, I recognized that I can transform my mind by meditating on the scriptures. For it is written, "Do not conform to the pattern of this world but be transformed by the renewing of your mind. Then you will be able to test and approve what God's will is—his good, pleasing and perfect will." (Romans 12:2 NIV) Transformation occured when I let go of everything including unpleasant situations, and kept believing that God's promises will manifest in my life according to his timing. It's God's job to do miracles, it's our duty to remain faithful and stand in selfless faith. This reminds me of what God told Abraham "All the land that you see I will give to you and your offspring forever."(Genesis 13:15 NIV) I had to daily transform my mind and heart in the way I receive, hear, and live according to the Word. I knew it was impossible for God to lie to me, so I began to walk as if I already received an answer to my prayers. Such radical faith is difficult and it requires daily dedication to studying the word of God to experience the fullness of the Holy Spirit.

To comfort myself when it became tiresome, I would think to myself, perhaps God was bragging on me the same way he did in the book of Job. "Then the Lord said to Satan, 'Have you considered my servant Job? There is no one on earth like him; he is blameless and upright, a man who fears God and shuns evil.'"(Job 1:8 NIV) Similar to Job's story, I passed the test and proved that I love God for who he is, not for what he gives me. I wasn't going to allow my lost of apartment cause me to break faith with God. My faith was absolutely not superficial, there was no giving up on God for me, because he allowed bad experiences. It is satan's strategy to get believers to doubt God's love for us when we encounter hardships, setbacks, or even unfair situations. God is capable of rescuing us from suffering, but he may also allow suffering to come for reasons we cannot understand. Life is not given merely for happiness or personal fulfilment but for us to serve and honor God. The worth and meaning of life is not based on what we feel, but on something that can't be taken away: our eternal gift of salvation, which we receive from Jesus Christ through faith. Never assume that God's love for us would block out suffering or pain; just keep the faith that God would never give you more than you can handle.

Job was a model of trust and obedience to God, yet the Lord permitted Satan to attack him in an especially harsh manner. Although God loves us, believing and obeying him do not shelter us from life's calamities. Setbacks, tragedies, and sorrow strike Christians and non-Christians alike. But in our tests and trials, God expects us to express our faith to the world. How do you respond to your troubles? Do you ask God, "Why me?" or do you say, "Use me LORD"? One of the most important lessons is being patient and fixing our eyes on Jesus during trials. Jesus cried out on the cross, but he never came down and fought his case. People must realize that a person's trials are not always a result of his or her own mistakes or sins. They can come about from other sources (such as spiritual warfare, generational curses, testing of faith etc.) We should learn from Job's experience to maintain patient, respectful, and loyal to God even in the midst of our sufferings (James 5:10-11). Seeing God's greatness and our own insignificance can help us to have a realistic perspective and to learn whatever lessons we can from each experience.

To suffer extreme loss, as Job did, was humiliating. I know how it feels to suffer in silence. When I came out to express what happened to me to share my vulnerability looking for comfort and support, I met lies, slander, and disrespect. Having my own "Job" moments, during my trials the Lord was teaching me patience, discipline, and perseverance. As I sought God for understanding the problems I was facing, and the Lord revealed a deep revelation of the Cross. I realized that I had to encounter much affliction to teach, witness to and give hope to people. Sometimes God allows pain to prepare us for a bigger assignment. During Calvary, Jesus took upon the sins of the world and his pain endured on the cross produced power. After his suffering, our saviour, Jesus Christ was exalted above every name on earth and heaven; He was crowned in glory. As disciples, we must identify with Christ — both in suffering and blessings. We should model mercy and love; just as Christ did. Thank God for his forgiveness for our sins, for Jesus had the power to call upon twelve legions of angels, (Matthew 26:53) but Jesus had to die to gain victory over Satan and sin. Jesus showed a perfect commitment to his Father's will. He would not advance the kingdom with swords, but with faith, love, and obedience. In my case, I needed self-forgiveness for letting things go too far in many areas of my life, including trying to change other people, being drawn into other people's dramas, thus giving my power away.

It's easy to be pulled into the turmoil of the world, which makes me think of Job again. In Job 1:1-3, we see a prime example of a righteous man who lost all his possessions, health, children, and flocks. He was not even respected for suffering bravely. Instead of his friends supporting him, they mocked, judged, and blamed him for his own sinfulness causing his troubles. They were wrong and God rebuked them later in the story.

There was a purpose to his struggles and pain and I trusted that God had a good plan for me. If God restored Job for his losses, I can be confident that he would do the same for me. (Job 42:10-17) Throughout the scriptures, Job refuses to give up on God even though he doesn't understand why he is facing trouble. Often we may feel beaten down, and tempted to turn from God, give up, and quit trusting him. There are important lessons we can learn from the book of Job. We should realize that a person's trials are not always a result of his or her own mistakes or sins. They can come about from other sources or other reasons, such as generational curses, faith tests, or using pressure to push us into our breakthrough. We should also learn from Job's experience to maintain patient respect and trust in God even during our sufferings (James 5:10-11). Seeing God's greatness and our own insignificance can help us have a realistic perspective and to learn whatever lessons we can from the experience. Satan was trying to curse Job but ended up pushing him into greater blessings, because of Job's unconditional love for God. He proved his faithfulness and continued to trust God, which is why Job was restored to wholeness.

Massive attacks are an indication that huge blessings are coming because the devil does not fight anything empty. So he tempts us and attacks us to try to push us further away from our blessings. Have you ever felt slandered, mocked, humiliated, and made the object of gossip? If so, keep your head up and never stop praying to God. Satan tried to slander

Job, but God knew that Job loved Him with true love. Job's faith wasn't based on his bank account, his health, his family, or anything else. Job genuinely loved God, he kept his faith alive in and continued to search for answers why bad things happen to good people. Likewise, for you, don't give in to defeat; Jesus is alive and well to fight all your battles if you believe. Job continued to trust and remain obedient to the Lord, yet God permitted Satan to attack him in an especially harsh manner. Although God loves us, believing and obeying him do not shelter us from life's calamities. Setbacks, tragedies, and sorrow strike Christians and non-Christians alike. But in our tests and trials, God expects us to express our faith to the world.

When your situation seems hopeless, determine that no matter how bad things become you will continue to pray, God will hear your prayers, and he will rescue you. When you send the word out over your life with faith, you're giving access to angels to work on your behalf. God promises us that is living word will not fall on the ground. "So is my word that goes out from my mouth: It will not return to me empty, but will accomplish what I desire and achieve the purpose for which I sent it." (Isaiah 55:11 NIV)

Often my difficult trials produced strength and greater confidence about the future. When the world seems like it's beating you down, when nothing seems like it ever goes right, when we are struggling to provide for our families, God still blesses us. When we are in despair, we call upon him for help without ever realizing that he is already carrying us. Everything we desire already exists within us. We must step into our truth and passion and greatness. The journey of wholeness has helped me recognize my strengths and weaknesses and build on my self-improvement. My journey was full of loss and transformation, but eventually led to hope. In time, I learned to be content in life and accept everything for what it is. For it is written, "But godliness with contentment is great gain" (1 Timothy 6:6 NIV). The more I honored God and centered my desire on him, the more I grew spiritually and in ever personal fulfillment. I learned how to live with less rather than desiring more. I may lose everything in life, but I kept God's vision and

His purpose for me deep within my heart. I had confidence that one day my hopes and dreams shall come to pass. Like Peter trying to walk on water, when I keep my eyes on the Lord, I'll always stay afloat, for I was under the watchful eyes of God.

CHAPTER 4

Seasons Change

Finally, able to move into my new house, I was starting to enjoy my new cozy living conditions. It was undeniably more spacious than my last apartment. This was the time to rebuild my career. I got a new full-time position as a pharmaceutical sales representative, and now I was making a better living. No more setbacks in my life, for Jesus has been gracious. I was the newest sales agent, and I exceeded sales objectives selling medication for pain, diabetes, and cardiovascular diseases.

From rags to riches, everything worked for me. God is marvelous! The Lord pours out favor and blessings that were so big that I forgot about my loss and pain of the past. It was such an honor to serve people and update physicians about new products that would help treat their patients. The best thing about this job was that it was flexible, and I had great communication with my team. Still, something was missing, and I had to make a major decision. Do I sacrifice my corporate job or devote myself full time to ministry? I stayed in sales for a year to save money and worked part-time in my fashion career; but this was only a temporary goal in order to be financially secured for working full-time in the ministry.

As I took on more fashion jobs, I noticed myself having less time in bible devotion with God. I starved my inner spiritual man, by overextending myself and not leaving enough time to study the word of God. Working two jobs, I was trying to secure financial stability and freedom, and when I got home I was exhausted. I read the bible every day before work, but my prayer life declined. Due to my hectic work schedule, I no longer stayed up at night to meditate on daily scriptures. I was trying to find a balance between working a corporate job, modeling, and planning church events. Every evening when I opened my bible, it seemed as if the spirit of slumber would capture me. I had a serious decision to make. Do I continue to chase financial security or do I let go and trust God's provision for me?

I know who it feels like to live in lack or abundance, regardless of the situation that I was facing it never changed my heart towards God. I was content whether I had plenty or whether I was in need. My secret was to draw on Christ's power for supernatural strength and trust God's promises. The key was to practice gratitude and avoid focusing on what I don't have. For God can take the smallest thing to multiply it, feeding a great multitude. An example would be in John 6 when Jesus highlighted his miracle power by multiplying five loaves and two fish to feed over 5000 people. Surprisingly, there were still left overs. (Luke 6:12) This scripture gives me the confidence to believe that God can use the scraps of something and increase it.

Never underestimate the power of God: it is when we give what we have in faith, especially when we have little, that he works on our behalf. Never falter in faith, when you are apprehensive about the troubles around you and doubt Christ's presence or ability to help, you must remember that he is the only one who can really help. When you begin to feel discouraged or defeated, remember that nothing is too hard for God. (Jeremiah 32:27).

Eventually, I could no longer work two jobs and work the ministry. Either my health, modeling gigs, corporate job, or ministry would suffer. I am only one person; perhaps this was my season of preparation for ministry. My situation was similar to in Luke 10:40-42, when Jesus teaches "But Martha was distracted by all the preparations that had to be made. She came to him and asked, "Lord, don't you care that my sister has left me to do the work by myself? Tell her to help me!" "Martha, Martha," the Lord answered, "you are worried and upset about many things, but few things are needed—or indeed only one. Mary has chosen what is better, and it will not be taken away from her."

In the passage above, we see that both Mary and Martha loved Jesus. On this occasion they were both serving him. But Martha thought Mary's style of serving was inferior to hers. She didn't realize that in her desire to serve, she was actually neglecting her guest. Are you so busy doing things for Jesus that you're not spending any time with him? Is Jesus still number one in your life? A distracted or busy christian is a defeated christian; every deed must be orchestrated by Jesus. If not, we could be laboring in vain. Despite of our challenges or responsibility; we must never lose the intimacy with Christ. As believers, we are to build our legacy with the Lord by daily seeking wisdom, council, and strength to do his will. Never let your service become self-serving; God gives us the grace and power to do things without overworking ourselves. As I reflect on my life, I've done good things at the wrong time. My fire and zeal for God made me work hard to spread the good news to the world, but it cost me losing what's most important: my personal time with myself and God. There will always be problems in the world, so some things can wait. We notice in the scriptures that Jesus didn't blame Martha for being concerned about household chores, but he was only asking her to set priorities. Service to Christ can degenerate into mere busy work that is no longer of devotion to God. Work for the king, but never miss the intimate moments of "being still and knowing" God. No one is a robot and we must have time to rest and recharge ourselves in the power of the Holy Spirit. Anointing is like a bank account; when we withdraw blessings to give to others, we then have to take time for God to deposit more dunamis power. Wholeness can only come from the presence of the Holy Spirit.

Jesus was my source of power, and I was determined to seek him no matter what. Having the attitude of dependence, our problems will drive us to God rather than away from him. Learn to rely on him daily.

Ultimately, serving requires us to focus on what he can do through us, not on what we can't do for ourselves. I needed a fresh touch from God again, so I needed to go back to my secret place again to recharge my spiritual batteries. I'm back on the road again to my holy mountain! When I arrived at my secret place I began to desperately seek God's face. This time I fell asleep on the mountain rock. I woke up to snakes, mosquitoes, and bugs on my legs. I jumped up immediately, and shook the poisonous viper off my leg. I had no major injuries, and I thanked God for protecting me. I fasted for seven days, with no food, only one gallon of water. I was determined to encounter a divine visitation from God. "Who may climb the mountain of the Lord? Who may stand in his holy place?" (Psalm 24:3 NIV)

I had to discipline myself and balance my life to be committed to consecrating myself unto the Lord and seek his face by any means. After consistent prayers, the next day, I saw three doves land next to me and dark clouds surround me with two light circles, that were shaped like eyes. I was shocked and trembling with fear. I seek God by reading the bible scriptures. Then, I boldly stood up with the bible in my right hand and poured out my heart to God. As I yelled, "I surrender to you God, take more of me, Lord, Give me more of your Holy Spirit." After crying out for more of God's presence and direction in my life, I was directed to read scripture that comforted me. I felt a new wind and peace in my heart. After this, I received a deep revelation from God, which increased my knowledge, understanding, and wisdom.

Inwardly, I changed dramatically. Although God didn't clarify the reason behind my experience of the fire, losing my job, and the tragic passing of my pet, I felt as if I had heaven on earth. I saw things from a different perspective; perhaps God was moving me out of my comfort zone. No defeat, only goodness and favor followed me.

Doing God's will sometimes means waiting patiently. While we wait, we can love on Jesus, serve others, and prepare for the work ahead of us. All things work in God's proper time. Everyone has a divine process, and I was never going to give up on my dreams but there were times when I wanted to rely on myself when God wanted me to depend on Him. Uncomfortable and full of uncertainty, I had no choice but to wait on the Lord to reveal more of his purpose and direction for my life. I wondered, "Why am I postponing my ministry to store up money?" I believed that my gifts would make a living for me, yet I feared starting a task and not having enough resources to complete it, which would be embarrassing. I felt a tug-of-war between making a good living and being called to the ministry. But I knew that I would rather be a slave for God than a tool for Satan. Money doesn't move me, God moves me. My true happiness will come when I reignite my fire and stir up my gifts and preach the gospel and make a difference in people' lives. Eventually, I made up my mind that no matter my situation, I refused to go back to the world or procrastinate on fulfilling my purpose, so I resigned from my job.

Tired of going back-and-forth with my thoughts, I had to move forward. I was no longer a victim of my circumstances, but I had to regain my personal power as a mighty warrior. I stood strong and commanded over my life, "I can do all things through Christ who strengthens me." (Philippians 4:13 NIV) Speaking God's living word over my life became a daily habit. Any time I felt lack, I knew just what I should speak over my life. The dunamis power received in union with Christ is sufficient to do his will and face all challenges in my life. God gave me the supernatural strength to do his will. As long as I continued to see with the eyes of faith I activated God's power in my life. I felt as if there were no limitations!

In chapter one, a preacher introduced me to the power of prayer and prophesied that God was going to use me as a mighty Prophetess to the nations. It was time for me to grow in the spirit and preach the gospel worldwide. If I sacrifice my job then I will be able to share my spiritual gifting to the world. I kept faith in God knowing he would provide all my needs according to the riches and glories. (Philippians 4:19) I trusted that my dreams for my ministry will come to pass. Then, I just needed to fully commit to the purpose that God had for me. I may have experienced many delays, including the apartment fire, but it was time to leave everything behind and devote myself to God. I had to give honor where it was due, and I decided to share my supernatural healing testimony with a preacher.

CHAPTER 5

Young Disciple in Formation

I visited the preacher to share my testimony for my supernatural healing of the ovarian cyst. That very day, while visiting the office, I committed wholeheartedly to serve in the ministry, and to grow in my spiritual life. The pieces of the puzzle were coming together, for God sent a servant to help me initate my ministry and give me some guidance in launching my first church. The preacher explained the importance of serving God and how a blessing is released when we are obedient to leadership. In Matthew 10:41-42 NIV it says, "Whoever welcomes a prophet as a prophet will receive a prophet's reward, and whoever welcomes a righteous person as a righteous person will receive a righteous person's reward. And if anyone gives even a cup of cold water to one of these little ones who is my disciple, truly I tell you, that person will certainly not lose their reward." This statement is true; how much we love God can be measured by how well we treat others. I like Jesus' illustration of giving a cup of cold water to a thirsty child because it shows a good model of unselfish service. Typically, a child can't or won't return a favor. God notices every good deed we do or don't as if he were the one receiving service. For it is written, "Serve wholeheartedly, as if you were serving the Lord, not people." (Ephesians 6:7 NIV) I was taught at a young age to provide my best service no matter what I may be doing because it displays good work ethics and would result to promotion. I was honored that God would send an angel ahead of me to guard and guide me to destiny. (Exodus 23:20)

This was all new. I was given instructions to prepare for training the next day at the church. Amazingly, my calling for ministry was similar to the call of Elisha (1 Kings 19:20), as I met a powerful minister who would assist me on my way to my destiny. The next day, I was given training on both biblical and practical topics. I spent time in intense bible training it was then my time to serve and learn the practical aspects of the work. This was my opportunity to showcase my prophetic gifts to the world. All that was required was faith in the living word. Jesus said it best when he taught, "Very truly I tell you, whoever believes in me will do the works I have been doing, and they will do even greater things than these, because I am going to the Father."(John 14:12 NIV) Jesus is saying here that his disciples working in the Holy Spirit would manifest the same giftings as long as they remained in faith. It's a faith connection. As long as I stayed connected to my source, which is the power of the Word, then all things would be possible.

I built my first church in Houston, Texas from the ground up, starting with only three people and a couple of ministers. Toward the end of the first month, we expanded to twelve people and started registering the organization. Starting this small church was difficult, yet God gave us the favor and grace to operate everything on such a tight budget. The money wasn't a real issue; it was the workers. We constantly prayed for God to give us workers to help fulfill his vision and plan for the ministry. It is vital that every missionary prays for new workers, for it isn't God's plan for us to work alone.

I knew that it required sacrifice in order to be great, therefore I abandoned everything that had given me false security, without looking back to the world. Nothing was going to distract me from following Christ Jesus. Daily, my team and I discussed strategies for how we would go into the world and reach the unreached people with the gospel of Jesus Christ. Under the guidance of an experienced preacher, I was performing in several roles; I was sometimes an usher, at times I was the janitor, but also I acted as a general overseer and administrator, often managing several departments. This was a great accomplishment for me at such a young age, and it was a lot of responsibility. And a lot of work.

Three times a week, I would drive one hour from my home to the church to set up music equipment. I would carry a 30 lb speaker on my back, which left me absolutely sore after installing the equipment. Unfortunately, the place that we were renting didn't have a safe storage place to leave the speaker, so I had to break them down and set them up for each service. Then, I would set up 500 chairs while I'm singing praises to the Lord. We were growing in members yet we were still on a tight budget. I had to wear many hats, from opening the church, setting up team meetings, editing and producing the sermon videos, overseeing the financial department, and serving the members.

I tried to get the workers involved with helping me clean the church and do other administrative work; however, it seemed as if no one was available. Therefore, I continued to work hard by myself and set up in time for the team to get there to meet at 7:00 am. Team meetings were set up for biblical teaching, church announcements and evangelism strategies. Afterward, I would speak with the team leader of each department and make sure that everything was running efficiently. I had no complaints because I was gaining great experience and I was a willing servant. I owe everything to God for love, mercy, healing, and most importantly, granting me salvation. Out of my appreciation for the Lord, I was fully committed to serve him and his people. Ultimately our agreement was to open church branches across the world and train leaders to oversee each church. By all means, I sacrificed everything to ensure that I kept my word to achieve our Heavenly Father's mandate.

Typically, around 8:00 am, I picked up people who didn't have transportation to get to church. This was my daily routine: it was very tiresome, yet it had to be done. After the service, I dropped off the team at home, then returned to the church to store the equipment. I must admit, it wasn't always easy managing a whole congregation. I enjoyed serving God, and this was the price I had to pay in order to keep things working smoothly. The church began to grow as the power of God manifested science and wonders throughout the congregation. The mighty power of the Holy Spirit used me and my team to do signs and wonders in healing the sick, restoring hearing to the deaf, curing HIV and cancer, and returning the lame to walk again. We even witnessed people jumping out of their wheelchairs. Hallelujah! Praise God! Testimony after testimony showed that God was still touching lives! It was my heart's desire to see God changing people's lives and I was able to witness the Holy Spirit live and direct. At the end of each day, I locked the doors of the church and drove to a park where I could meditate and relax for the rest of the evening. It was such a great honor to be given the opportunity to serve God and learn the ministry work.

I was honored that God connected me with amazing people that were on fire for God. We were able to make a huge impact in the communities. It amazed me how much we were able to accomplish, when we had the same vision and we were all cooperating to serve Jesus' purpose and not take the credit for ourselves: which is to spread the gospel to mankind. It is vital that believers tell others about the salvation that is available to everyone through faith in Jesus Christ. Are you ambitious for God? What are you willing to sacrifice for God? Is your desire, more than anything else, to please God and to do his will? One simple way to test your commitment to Christ is in your serving. We don't serve God for blessing; but we serve God because we love him and have compassion for his people.

A key member of the team has to leave us, but we carried on running our church. I continued to preach, evangelize, and operate the ministry full-time in Houston. In the next chapter, I have to make a major decision that would shift my life forever, either for better or worse.

CHAPTER 6

Faith Over Fear

After praying in my secret place, at my prayer mountain, the Lord showed me a vision of ministering on stage to a very diverse crowd. Perhaps this was the crusade and revival that I had consistently been praying for. A very vivid vision, it seemed as if I were in a foreign country. A few minutes later I received a call, inviting me to come to another country and preach. Perhaps this call was not a coincidence, I thought to myself, "This is definitely a confirmation of the vision that I have received." I hesitated to tell say "Yes" because it was like starting my life completely over. Later, I was told that "Many are called, but few are chosen" (Matthew 22:14 NIV). I was urged not to look back to worldly stability or comfort. I thought to myself, "What is the worst that can happen? I must not be afraid of the unknown, so I listened to that advice and took a leap of faith. I already prepared myself financially for the new journey, so I rented out the church in Houston, Texas to my sister in the Lord. She was a very kind-hearted woman of God that would Pastor the congregation, while I focused on managing the two international churches.I was excited to be chosen to setting up healing revivals internationally, and be a featured guest speaker on television and radio.

Apprehensively, I agreed to travel to Africa to be a part of the program, joining in missionary work and participating in revivals. I was happy but a little scared of traveling to a new country by myself. I chose faith over fear, and immediately I transferred funds to sponsor this new assignment as well as my living arrangements. I had to push myself out of my comfort zone, for opportunities like this would not last forever. In the end, I knew God was with me so I took a bold approach. I chose to step out on faith in this new journey.

Experience is the best teacher, and working in the ministry has taught me how to walk in the power of God: selflessly, courageously and mercifully. My secret of walking in the heavy anointing is love, forgiveness, and sacrifice in serving others. Love manifests itself in giving, therefore sacrificing your time in serving others faithfully is considered as one of the greatest deeds, in God's eyes. For it is written, the greatest among you will be your servant. (Matthew 23:11) I was devoted to serving the people, all for the glory of God. From an early age, my mother always taught me to give myself to serving others, even when it hurts. Self-sacrificing and serving kept me aware of other's needs and helped me prevent becoming prideful. As believers, we are not to only love with words, but in deeds. As Christians, we are to move into the world serving God and each other. We should never become arrogant in our serving or great deeds, for all glory belongs to the Lord.

Life is similar to a classroom; it is full of tests and the open-book cheatsheet is the bible. Often difficult circumstances help equip us and tap into our talents, gifts, and passions that are given to us from God. Yet, it is the leading of the Holy Word that grants us success in life! I am trained and qualified by the King of Glory.

Whether good or bad circumstances, our service should bring glory and honor to God. When we understand the perspective of God, then competition is not a factor and we can appreciate each other's gifts, celebrate one another, and bring glory back to our Heavenly Father. The secret to serving in humility and confidence is, instead of comparing yourself to your neighbor, constantly compare yourself to Jesus Christ, and boast on his righteousness and his perfection. There is no one on earth that is perfect as the Holy Lamb of God. (Romans 3:23)

My life hasn't always been easy; however he gave the wisdom from experience, combined with scriptures. Through trials and tribulations, it is necessary to understand how others feel and to provide a solution to their problems, based on what you went through and the experience you gained. Through suffering, I've been able to be a beacon of light for others. Long-suffering, is a fruit of the Spirit, and difficulties and discomfort are typically associated with higher advancement in Christ's Kingdom.

To show my commitment to the work of God, I immediately donated all of my belongings in my home and put the house on the market for rent. I drew my confidence from the word in Luke 18:29-30 NIV, "Truly I tell you, Jesus said to them, "no one who has left home or wife or brothers or sisters or parents or children for the sake of the Kingdom of God will fail to receive many times as much in this age, and in the age to come eternal life." I was willing to pay the high price to leave my home and career to follow Jesus. Salvation is free but the anointing will cost you everything. Jesus demands a sacrifice in serving him, for we should never get comfortable in a particular environment, and we should always have the zeal to spread the good news of salvation. There were benefits as well as sacrifices required, but I wasn't going to settle for a comfortable life. I never dwelt on what I have given up because I can never out-give God, for I was born for this! I knew the best was yet to come as long as I stayed focused on my new assignment. After boldly making this faith decision, God granted me the favor to find a tenant to move into my house and pay rent for two years. Everything was going great, and now it was my time to step out on my new journey.

I left the United States. After landing in my destination, while walking to the taxi, I began to hear loud gunshots. Immediately, I opened the car door and ducked down under the seat and earnestly prayed for protection over our lives. I believed that God would not let us die before our time. I have no fear of death. No matter what happens, I had to trust that be courageous and not allow dangerous conditions to hinder my assignment. I made a vow to serve God forever, nothing will stop my assignment on earth. Every day, I strive to live a holy devoted life to Christ without allowing external circumstances to weaken my faith. Five minutes later, the shooting stopped. We were so close to the shooting, It was under the shadow of the Lord's wing that protected us (El Shaddai, the Lord of protection). I told myself, "I am under the watchful eyes of God." Praise God! Faith changes everything. After this event, I begin to be boldness to conquer the fear of death.

"Even though I walk through the darkest valley, I will fear no evil, for you are with me; your rod and your staff, they comfort me." (Psalm 23:4 NIV) There are times when death casts a frightening shadow over us because we may seem entirely helpless in the present situation. We may struggle with enemies of pain, injury, disease, suffering- but supernatural strength and courage cannot overcome death. It is only when we walk through the death's dark valley when we can grow in deeper trust of God majestic dunamis power.

God has given all human beings the emotion of fear as a warning of danger, but we are not supposed to have so much that it immobilizes us and keeps us from serving God as we should. Timothy 1:7-8 NIV declares, "God has not given us a spirit of fear." Fear paralyzes us and keeps us from wielding the authority we have in Christ to bring healing to others. Also in John 5:18, it teaches us that without God permission "the wicked one does not touch [whoever is born of God]" (see also Luke 10:19 NIV). Whenever things are going well and you're really close to your goal, you may become complacent, but that's exactly when the enemy feels threatened and strikes; people have suffered a backlash from the enemy when they are engaged in spiritual warfare, which causes the feeling of fear. The problem comes when you give in to fear, it becomes a spiritual prison and locks you out of your purpose; faith opens the doors to unlimited access to opportunities. If you led by the Holy Spirit, you can overcome any demonic backlash and Satan no longer has a legal right when you are operating in faith through Jesus Christ. Faith brings God on the scene; fear blocks God from operating in your life. Yet, if we are led by Christ then we are covered by the word of God. Luke 12:32 gives us wise counsel: "'Do not be afraid, little flock, for it is your Father's good pleasure to give you the kingdom.'"

When I boldly spoke the word of God, I changed my reality. It is the Spirit who gives life; the flesh profits nothing. The words that I speak to you are a spirit, and they are life. (John 6:63). Make sure your words are aligning to God words, never speak of defeat. Whatever you believe is what you get. (Proverbs 23:13) Always walk in faith, and trust God's promises over your life. Faith activated heaven's miracle power in our life. For it is written, the just shall live by faith. (Hebrews 10:38) Hearing the word of God benefits Christians because it's necessary to speak the word in faith during temptation and trials. Jesus was able to overcome the devil in the wilderness by understanding and applying the word in his life. (Matthew 4:1-11) If a believer doesn't hear the word of God, there are prone to be deceived by the devil lies. We only build strong faith by hearing the word of God. So then faith must come by hearing by the word of God. (Romans 10:17)

As Christians, we should always walk by faith and in the expectancy that God has directed our paths. "However, when the spirit of truth comes, he will lead you into all the truth." (John 16:13) In the Bible, "faith" means believing in God, and in what Christ has done for us to make our salvation possible–and then committing ourselves to Him. We are righteous of Christ Jesus. In other words, faith has two parts to it, and both are equally important. The first part is believing in God and that He loves us and sent His Son into the world to save us. Faith isn't a vague hope that God might exist; it is a definite belief that what the Bible says about Him is true. The Bible says, "Without faith, it is impossible to please God." (Hebrews 11:6 NIV) The second part of faith is a commitment–a definite decision not only to believe in our minds that Christ can save us but to put our lives into His hands and trust Him alone for our salvation. True faith not only believes Christ can save us but actually trusts Him to do it. Faith and prayer intertwine together as an agreement to the Word of God.

My faith-- exercising both parts-- kept me going in my Kingdom assignments. Living and adjusting to a new climate and environment was extremely different from America. Due to the change in food and water, I experienced malaria for the first two weeks of my journey.

Still preaching with a high fever; my passion continued to propel me to keep my commitment to my assignment. There was nothing to make me stop because I didn't want to let my leaders down. The next day, the church family urged me to take time for myself. They showed love and appreciation for my loyalty and commitment, but I had to rest. So, I sat out for a couple of weeks for my full recovery. After supplemental drinks and eating daily bread; I gained back my strength. Glory to God! I made up my mind that nothing would avert my assignment.

My labor was not in vain. God blessed me to fund and assist in building two international churches. I had achieved my biggest dream. At every team meeting, I gathered the congregation together to pray that God would provide us more resources to expand our Kingdom assignment worldwide, which is to provide healing and the good news of the gospel throughout the world. Daily my prayer was, "Father, use me as a channel of blessing for your people". As I reminisce on life, the Lord has shown me amazing grace; I went from the world's model to God's spokesmodel. My mission was to bring hope to the hopeless. This wasn't just a building; it was a spiritual house for providing solutions to people's living problems. I felt the presence of God working mightily upon me. Similar to the Apostle Paul in Acts 5:15, I would walk past people and the *dunamis* power on me would often cause miracles and healings to occur. In fact, during a church service, God used me to bring about a supernatural healing of an elderly lady from throat cancer, which she happily testified about the next day. Shocked, I kneeled down and praised God for using me in such a way. For it is written, "For the kingdom of God is not a matter of talk but of power" (1 Corinthians 4:20 KJV).

My joy came from spreading love and providing hope. As I began to travel for missionary assignments, witnessing poverty in certain areas made my heart heavy. I would begin to weep to see hungry children in the streets and no one showing love or compassion. Perhaps, there was so much poverty, that people became blind to that level of destitution. The sight of dead bodies in the middle of the street left me disturbed for several weeks. This distressing event imprinted on my mind and heart because I had nightmares of seeing the dead people in my dreams for four days. It is very important that we guard what our eyes see. I would advise Christians to avoid watching violent or disturbing images that could subconsciously negatively affect the mind. It could come from movies, music, or even video games. By God's grace, my mind was cleansed through the precious blood of Jesus Christ and I was no longer scared by the trauma caused by disturbing images and other terrible sights I have seen in life.

Even though it was dangerous on the streets, we didn't allow fear to stop us from evangelizing the good news of the gospel or participating in community events. My team and I were committed to helping put together a program to feed all the hungry people in the street. Life is all about being selfless and focusing on blessing others that are less fortunate. The Bible tells us," Let your light so shine before men, that they may see your good works, and glorify your Father in Heaven (Matthew 5:16 NIV). Christian faith is not about speaking of or hearing about scriptures, but it's about being a doer of the word (James 1:22). We want to walk the walk and not just talk the talk. These people's problems were serious; we were dealing with life and death issues, and I was there to offer hope. After seeing so much suffering, my team made it my propriety to help people with the blessings God has given me. Obedience to God's instructions made me available to help others and make a difference in the world.

As my team and I continued to work toward building our new church, we found more land and commercial buildings for sale. God blessed us with a huge piece of land where we started constructing a building that could hold approximately 2,500 people. My mission was to reach the unreached, speaking the Good news of the salvation of Jesus Christ and healing hurting souls, globally. Everything was going great until I receive a long distance call from my mother, who was weeping. Later, I learned that there was a death in my family. My church family wanted me to stay and work in the ministry; however, I couldn't just leave my mother comfortless. I chose to travel back to Houston to get my house in order. My entire team comfort me and urged me to go back home to take care of myself as well as my family. All the team leaders assured me that someone would oversee the congregation until I returned. They assured me that I would always have a home there and we would be connected. The next day, my church family gave me hugs and sweet words of encouragement as they dropped me off at the airport.

CHAPTER 7

Broken Vessel

After traveling to my mother's side, she maintained a show of strength, but deep inside, I knew she was grieving. I thought to myself, "If only I had been there during this difficult time to uplift her spirits, she would not be so downhearted." I constantly encouraged my mother and tried to take her outdoors, thinking that a change of scenery would help her recharge her emotional state. It was a hard pill to swallow-- in the same month, I lost two close loved ones. All I could do was remain strong and positive; I focused on planning a funeral and gathering everyone for prayers. I didn't show it, but the death took a great hold on my life. I smiled and stayed strong around my family, but deep inside I felt heartache. I kept speaking the Word over my life, which gave me the confidence and strength to go on effectively. I had to do a self-deliverance over my life, casting out all spirits of guilt that lingered from feeling disconnected from my mother. There was a part of me that died, both spiritually and mentally. In my grief, I didn't have the motivation to continue to do ministry. Checking in with the team leaders overseas, I let them know that I had business to attend to in the US and would need some time and they assured me that everything was fine. I felt so blessed that my serving was not in vain and my leader helped me raise up other disciples to oversee my department until my return.

During this time, I experienced some resistance from my friends in my church community and was unduly criticized and slandered for some online videos I had posted. This caused controversy among some of my closest allies, which hurt me deeply due to my vulnerable state of grief. Unfortunately, I found myself alone and without anyone to turn to. As much as I would have liked for friends to comfort me, no one was available for me. When my emotional pain overwhelmed me, I longed for companionship. If only people would understand my situation and work with me to improve it. If only I had a team or support system; I was looking for someone to put human flesh on God's comfort. This may sound unspiritual to most people, but it's the truth. In the darkest moments, Jesus, too wanted his friends to pray for him. In Mark 14:32-34 NIV, They went to a place called Gethsemane, and Jesus said to his disciples, "Sit here while I pray." He took Peter, James, and John along with him, and he was deeply distressed and troubled. "My soul is overwhelmed with sorrow to the point of death," he said to them. "Stay here and keep watch." But they fell asleep, and they were not responsive to Jesus' request.

It the scripture above, we can understand how Jesus didn't want to be left alone in his suffering. He was seeking human companionship from his disciples. There was a time when Jesus was alone and communing with his Father, and there was a time when he wanted to feel support from friends. Likewise, I have clung to friends for comfort, when I was healing from my broken heart, but I learned that all I needed was Jesus' presence; his fellowship and love healed my heart. Yet, there is a friend that sticks closer than a brother (Proverbs 8:24), and his name is Jesus. No one has ever transformed me or inspired me the way the scripture has. I was strengthened by the power of the word, for there is no better love than Jesus', and it encouraged me to continue to work on my goals. Neither my family nor friends could ever give me the healing I desperately needed. God's presence is like heaven. Nothing in the world could satisfy my soul but Jesus Christ. All I needed was a touch or a hug from the inside, from the divine one.

Based on my experience, the emotional pain of losing a loved ones cuts deeply and pierces the heart, leaving you bleeding for several weeks or even months. It feels as if there are sharp aches and pains through the heart.The good news is there is one thing that brings us hope in the midst of anything and that is Jesus. With the help of my comforter, the Holy Spirit, I was able to overcome all of my trials.

It was time for me to be strong and move on in life, leaving everything in God's hands! When we allow God to take control of our lives, we will find ourselves walking in joy, peace, love, and contentment, which will make anxiety a thing of the past. Although I knew God's direction for my life, I had to find a way to balance myself. Healing is a process but I expected it to come overnight. Even though I was willing to walk away and start anew, I was plagued with worries: Why do the good die? How did I lose myself? Why are my friends rejecting me? The Lord know what transpired in my life, and all I could do was trust the process by moving on.

Perhaps many have had the sad experience of losing family, friends, or feeling isolation that can leave people crippled by their loss. Even as adults, the pain may linger. It's best to trust God word and allow him to take first place in our life, fill that void, and heal that hurt. Jesus can take the role of a Father or Mother for us. His love is sufficient for all our needs. Jesus healed my broken heart.

Due to unexpected circumstances, my partners in Africa and I decided to part ways. We just decided to go our separate ways and they took care of the churches in Africa and I turned my attention to my new ministry in the US. This reminds me of the Genesis story of Abraham and Lot; our season was over and we part ways in peace. Although I was a little nervous heading into an unknown situation and having to step out in faith and rebuild my life all over again, I was not going to be deterred. I literally had to start over, but it had to be in God's time, not mine. Things were taking longer than I thought and I grew frustrated. I often became angry because of delays, limited resources and hardships. My desire to fulfill my purpose was so great, but obstacles continued to hinder my progress, and my frustration increased and took hold of me. I often thought, "What's the point of living is you can't fulfill your dreams? I shed many tears waiting for my opportunity to share my gifts with the world. Desperately, crying out to God, "Save now, I beseech you, O Lord: O Lord, I beseech you, send now prosperity." (Psalm 118:25 KJV) There are the days when the last thing we want to do is rejoice. Our mood is down, our situation is out of hand, and our sorrow, anger, or guilt is overwhelming. My response was with righteous anger. I often told myself, "My situation must change."

Righteous anger is controlled anger that is motivated by compassion and not by ego. When confronting sinful behaviour or injustice, always align with the Word because you remain in integrity when you speak up for truth. Don't jeopardize your duty as a disciple to speak in love and truth; never compromise your faith in order to fit in with the crowd. Be on fire for your beliefs. By standing up for righteousness, you are honoring God's Word over popularity; likewise when you don't act, you dishonor God. For it is written, Whoever is ashamed of me and my words, the Son of Man will be ashamed of them when he comes in his glory and in the glory of the Father and of the holy angels. (Luke 9:26) Whenever you're in a situation where somebody is making a wrong decision and you refuse to stand up, you're hiding your light-- whether the situation calls for anger, or tears, or grieving. Did you know that confronting sinful behavior is an act of compassion? Whenever you have anger to hurt someone that is ego-driven, this is a sin, but anger to stop injustice is appropriate.

I want to encourage you that no matter how low you get in life, never let that situation stop you from expressing your honest concerns and conversation with the Lord. For it is written, "Cast your burden on the Lord, and he will sustain you. He will never allow the righteous to be moved."(Psalm 55:22 NIV) God wants us to cast our cares on him, but often we continue to try to carry the weight of the world on our shoulders, instead of leaving everything in God's hands. Trust the same strength that sustains you to carry your cares as well, for the Lord Almighty is faithful. Based on my experience, the Lord has been my mind's regulator, keeping me at perfect peace. It only takes one encounter with God, then everything is alright.

I trusted God with my life wholeheartedly, I wasn't going to allow my frustration or not being able to change a situation to overtake me. Patience is a virtue, yet it's not an easy thing to do, especially when you're under pressure. Every time I would feel peace within, I experienced more spiritual attacks that distracted me. I desperately wanted a change in my life. Once again, righteous anger began to build up within my spirit, and I began to pray fervently with argumentative prayers, and I was constantly asking God questions: What are you trying to show me? Why are you taking so long? Am I'm worthy of love and support? I kept trusting that my best days were ahead of me, and I knew that whatever was meant for me would flow into my life effortlessly.

Surely and steadily, I was building again and I was trusting God to provide for me every step of the way; and he was faithful to answer my prayers. God was loyal, merciful, and gracious to me. I was never lacking anything during my new journey. My faith and strength were getting stronger, also I was able to witness some miraculous encounters with Jesus. I realized that all I need in life was the favor of God, I didn't need to trust in any idols in my life, such as money, people, or my own abilities. I fell into the hands of my Lord, fully depending on his love and grace. " For I know the plans I have for you," declares the LORD, "plans to prosper you and not to harm you, plans to give you hope and a future."(Jeremiah 29:11 NIV) No longer would I have to stress, worry, or have anxiety about my future.

My main focus was to fulfill God's purpose for my life, and I had made many changes in my surrender that were difficult for me to adjust to. I allowed everything to fall apart, including myself. I felt like a had a spiritual death due to my deep depression that came as a result of me giving into doubts. "Many are the afflictions of the righteous: but the Lord delivereth him out of them all." (Psalm 34:19 KJV) We often wish we can escape troubles, the pain of grief, loss, sorrow, frustration, and failure. God promises to be close to the brokenhearted, to be our source of power, courage, wisdom, and by helping us during our problems. When trouble strikes, don't be dismayed. God is big enough to handle any difficulties. For it is written, "I am the LORD, the God of all mankind. Is anything too hard for me?"(Jeremiah 32:7 NIV) Trust doesn't always come easy, but it is necessary to unlock the hidden blessings of God. Do you ever feel overwhelmed, full of worries, fearful or hopeless? If so, find your strength in Christ. Don't be afraid to pour out your heart to God, humbly admit that you need his supernatural provision and trust that he will perfect his Word in your life. I can testify that no matter how low life brings you, Jesus will always stand by your side.

During my healing process, I was able to let go of my pain, fear, and depression and lay every burden at the feet of Jesus. God gave me hope, confidence, and courage to stand alone in the midst of losing my loved ones. I learned that when I felt discouraged, I should not have withdrawn myself from others. Being isolated caused me to sink deeper into depression and allowed discouragement to come in. I wanted to be alone. I spent all my time soaking in the presence of Jesus, listening to intimate songs of worship. There is always beauty in the ashes; my heart was broken as a way to tear down my wall of protection, to comfort me, and through full surrender, God's healing power could enter. It amazed me how God loved unconditionally and continually and never let me go. He pulled me in close and showed me love that I had never known. I was blessed to be able to experience deeper aspects of the Father's heart for me. By the grace of God, I found the strength to rise up from my fall and start over.

I am not ashamed of my scars in life because they made me stronger, wiser, and have helped me find my healing power from within. Most importantly, I share in the same suffering as Christ Jesus. I am proud of my scars because they speak courage, and they show others what I've bravely endured. This reminds me of John 20:24-27 when Thomas (Jesus' disciple) asked Jesus to show him the nails in his hands. Scars or brokenness provide an opportunity for God's power to be displayed. On the positive side, my affiliations drew me into a deeper intimate relationship with Jesus. God healed my broken heart and gave me the strength to continue to walk in the power of supernatural love. The Holy Spirit was with me guiding, protecting, comforting, and showering love on me. All my challenges gave me the confidence to boldly live in the power of Jesus Christ's grace. No matter how low I sank, God was willing to heal and lift me up again. I was living in the overflow of God's presence. My heart was burning for Jesus; I hoped this deep peace would stay with me forever.

I was entering a new season of blessing, I told myself. Following God's instructions, I let go of everything and fully surrendered to God for the plan for my life. I never lost my confidence, but I didn't have the fiery passion for my dreams like I did in the past. All I could do is look up for God to reignite my passions and desires to live out my dreams again. My hope was coming back alive, I felt a spark and fire in my heart again. Jesus was up to something, but he only revealed the details to me in pieces, like a puzzle. I believe that my story will have a beautiful ending. For it is written, "Being confident of this, that he who began a good work in you will carry it on to completion until the day of Christ Jesus." (Philippians 1:6 NIV) At this time, the only thing that I depend on was the Word of God. I believed that I would see God's good work in me continue throughout my lifetime and I would finish it when I meet him face to face in paradise.

CHAPTER 8

Worthy

Although scarred, after all of this loss, I still trusted that I am uniquely worthy. The cross reminds me of the beauty and holiness of Christ Jesus. God chose not to erase the marks of death during the crucifixion on Calvary. In fact, the wounds and scars represent the unconditional love and forgiveness he has for humanity. There is a price for being identified with Jesus, but I share in his glory and sufferings. (Romans 8:17) Therefore, I'm not ashamed of being bruised for, I get to partake in the glory and power of the Resurrection. I believe my scars are beautiful; our suffering is nothing compared to the great price that Jesus paid to provide salvation for me.

As I focused on the power of the cross, something stirred in me. I was more sensitive to the spirit; my life has been a shadow of Jesus Christ's life. I was able to overcome the sting of rejection by keeping my mind renewed in the scriptures. As I compare my life to Jesus' life, I want to give people the courage to overcome opposition, shame, and suffering. Eventually the Lord restored my dreams and passions; now I have the spiritual vision and strength to look past my own suffering to my eternal life in Heaven. (Hebrews 12:2). I would not allow shame or rejection by others to cause me to lose community with Christ. I had to lose my life to find God's complete divine purpose for my life. I'm glad for all the adversity because it has made me ten times stronger than before. Jesus is my glory and strength, and the word overwhelmingly confirms that I am his cherished possession. God's love is relentless, immeasurable, and infinite; for I have everything I need.

My trials came, in part, from me showing my soft side as a minister. It takes courage to admit that you're hurting from suffering a loss, and instead of acting tough and putting up a good front. But I want to inspire others to feel free to express their vulnerabilities and to continue to fight for what they believe in. Being a minister, I was led to believe that I had to act like I was perfect, but I went against popular opinion and wanted to be an example for others to feel comfortable in their skin and process their emotions in a healthy way. Don't be afraid to humbly express yourself, for the anointed ones cry as well. For it is written, " Jesus wept." (John 11:35 NIV) You may cry, you may scream, you may crawl to the finish line, but never give up on your dreams: if I made it through, then so can you.

I must admit, there were moments when I allowed my emotions to supersede my intelligence. I am very passionate and sometimes I openly express deep and strong feelings for hurting souls and for kingdom work. I was ridiculed for making heartfelt sermons about love and forgiveness, and perhaps my message was too sensitive for the male listener. However, I received great feedback from the female listeners. All that matters is that lives are being impacted and changed for the best. My only concern was to lead people to Christ, I just wanted to bring broken souls to the Kingdom of God. I can relate to what Paul states in 1 Corinthians 9:22-23 NIV, "To the weak I became weak, to win the weak. I have become all things to all people so that by all means I might save some." I do all this for the sake of the gospel, that I may share in its blessings.

My goal was to make common ground with everyone I come in contact with, making them feel comfortable to be themselves, and feel accepted, being sensitive to their needs and concerns, and looking for a solution to share the gospel of Jesus Christ. While this never means compromising my faith or taking part in sin. God would use my kindness to bring sinners into repentance. I wasn't concerned about being foolish in people's eyes, I just wanted to glorify God. Deep inside I have a tender heart, but a tough mind. When I was going through various trials, many of my brothers and sisters in the church advised me to hide it; they told me that telling the truth will destroy my ministry. However, I did the opposite of what they advised me, because overcoming my trials may give hope to someone that felt like giving up on their dreams. I wasn't going to bury my pain and failure, but I was going to share it with others in order to give hope to people going through similar situations.

There is nothing wrong with releasing the truth with love. I wanted to share my vulnerability to testify the goodness of God, by sharing my testimony of his amazing resurrection power. I couldn't be a hypocrite or refuse to give honor and glory to my Lord Jesus. I will lose popularity to boost my weakness so that Christ would be glorified in my life. (2 Corinthians 12:9) My debility helps me develop maturity and grow stronger in my Christian character. It also develops a deeper intimacy for God because I was relying on the Lord's strength for the weak area in my life. When we feel weak, allowing God to fill us with his power, then we are stronger than we could ever be on our own. God doesn't intend for us to seek to be weak, passive, or ineffective- life provides enough hindrances and setbacks without us creating them. When those obstacles come, we must depend on God. Only his power will make us effective for him and will help us do the work that has lasting value. My life has been proof of the Father's love, for I was healed and loved back to life. I'm thankful for God anointing the areas of my weaknesses so he could show himself strong in my life. I have no regrets; I am worthy because I am the righteousness of God. Everyone's cross of suffering is different. Embrace your scars and walk in supernatural love. I am who I am by the special grace of God, therefore I wore my scars like jewels, something I treasured to remind me of everything I have endured. Pain produces power and wisdom, I will never hide my scars. Often, I wonder if the only signs of sin in heaven will be the scars in Jesus' hands, feet, and side. This will be a reminder forever and forever that our blessed Lord paid the price for our redemption. Glory be to God Almighty.

Shame and disgrace could no longer dictate my worthiness when I discovered the beauty in my ashes. It's such a beautiful exchange and so amazing how the Lord takes ashes and turns them to beauty. In the past, sometimes I would self-sabotage, thinking I've made too many mistakes and there is no hope for me. Sometimes I allowed frustration to take over me because I desperately wanted a change and was tired of long-suffering. God constantly encouraged me and reminded me of how valuable I am to him, even when I didn't feel worthy. I saw myself as an abandoned puppy that God picked up by the scruff of the neck, to bring me home — comforting me and reassuring me I was not alone. After this vision, I felt refreshed, appreciated, and worthy to have the King of the universe looking down on me with the eyes of mercy to inspire me to complete his will. I felt humbled, thinking, "Who am I that the Lord constantly watches over and searches to find me when I feel lost, discouraged, or confused?" Amazing grace deems me worthy no matter what. I thank God for making the "unqualified" qualified through grace.

I was far from perfect, but I knew the Lord was my director. Occasionally, worrisome thoughts would arise, such as, "How can I be a blessing to the people if they associate me with my damaged past, instead of seeing the strength in that. Will my weaknesses get in the way of my ministering to people?" Even in these times of insecurity, I held onto my deep belief that God knew what was best for me; I just had to trust and keep planting the seeds of love and hope. Based on the Word, I knew that I was worthy and I can remain confident I'm a golden vessel, ready for the Master to use. I no longer felt shame or unworthiness about my past mistakes. "There is no condemnation for those who are in Christ Jesus." (Romans 8:1 NIV) I learned to just accept everything for what it is, no one is perfect. God has me in his loving arms and I am under the watchful eyes of God.

CHAPTER 9

Burned out but Blessed

The spiritual path isn't often a straight line, there are ebbs and flows, lush periods and parched ones. At one point, I found myself in a spiritual desert. Questions lingered in the back of my mind. Has God forgotten about me? Is this a faith test? I feel like my life is an emotional rollercoaster. In the past, I felt a deep connection with the Holy Spirit, but suddenly I felt as though something stuck me in a wilderness. I didn't feel a deep presence of God, now the only thing I was living by was my faith in his Word. No longer did I feel the power of God upon me, yet I knew that the Holy Spirit lived inside of me. The more I prayed and spoke in tongues, the less I felt a connection. I wanted to have the mountain top experience again, which was the passionate desire and heart blazing on fire. All I could do was to wait patiently on the Lord. "Be still and know that he is God." (Psalm 46:10 KJV) I learned to take it one day at a time, without rushing, to be still and wait on God to give me prophetic directions on my next journey. Waiting and being content is one of the most painful parts of fulfilling destiny. During this time, I had to keep repeating to myself, "Patience is a virtue." "Godliness with contentment is a great gain." (1 Timothy 6:6 NIV) I learned to trust God's unfailing love even when he's silent; his timing is the best. In John 11, the Lazarus story teaches us that all things work out perfectly in God's timing (especially his delays). Keep the faith in believing that the Lord needs will be manifested on the perfect schedule and purpose. We must continue to work hard, pray, trust, and await his timing.

Although I continually walked boldly into my calling, I felt impatient, wanting bigger things to happen faster. Often I felt like similar to the widow in Luke 18:5 NIV, who kept begging the judge, "Grant me justice against my adversary." I persisted in prayers and refused to give up my faith fight, and I had to keep working and crying out to God until something happened. Perhaps, God wasn't sitting me on a shelf; he may have been delaying me for a good reason. I noticed that as I personally prayed for changes in my circumstances, I began to grow in character, faith, and hope. Referring back to Luke 18:5 NIV when the judge says, "Yet because this widow keeps bothering me, I will see that she gets justice so that she won't eventually come and attack me!'"This brings a great question to my mind. If an unjust judge responded to constant pressure, how much more will a great and loving Savior respond to us? If we know he loved us, we can believe he will hear our cry for help. Never lose hope, our King Jesus is faithful.

Nothing good comes easy; there's a divine process I had to go through. I may have lost everything from a physical standpoint, but I had the Holy Spirit within me. Therefore, I have everything that matters. For it is written, "Greater is him that lives in me than in the world." (1 John 4:4 NIV). I went from great highs to great lows. It seemed as if my spiritual battery had burned out. How could I recharge myself? Nothing seemed to work, the only thing I could do was continue to put my hope in the word of God. "For no word from God will ever fail" (Luke 1:37 NIV) Perhaps God was putting me in this situation so that I would rely only on the word of God and not need to feel the Holy Spirit. Sometimes I sensed distance from God, and every time I prayed there was no change. All my prayers seemed to be bouncing off the wall. After fasting and praying earnest prayers, God didn't change my situation. I was overcome with emotional sickness. I thought God left me, so I went back to the secret place where I first found God. Gracefully, I could reconnect to God. Then, I was refreshed and recharged again in my spirit.

After spending time in prayer, God revealed he wanted me to grow deeper in my faith. In fact, his silence was necessary to train my ears to hear clearer and sharpen my spiritual eyes to see. This allowed me, as a believer to increase confidence and trust in the promises of God when everything is showing the opposite. "We walk by faith and not by sight." (2 Corinthians 5:7 NIV) When I walk according to the world, my perspective is through carnal eyes, which caused me to feel in despair; I had to keep my eyes fixed Jesus Christ, which filled me with hope. Being optimistic, I continued to stand and speak life into my current situation. I knew that it was impossible to fail when faith is present. I could not give up on God's vision, and I had to keep fighting the good fight of faith. "Let us hold unswervingly to the hope we profess, for he who promised is faithful." (Hebrews 10:23 NiV) I knew my suffering was not in vain and that God would come through for me. I was praying out of desire and frustration to fulfill my assignment from my current situation. I didn't feel that I had enough to pull off my dream of building a church. In fact, occasionally I had argumental prayers with the Lord. Such as, "How can I be a blessing if I don't have the resources?" God told me to start where I am and use what is right in front of me. Fair and righteously that God is, he would give me a strategy on how I could make an impact for his Kingdom. Courage, honesty, faith, and love is the key to unlock the blessings of God.

Living in the power of God, I experienced a spiritual high. I suddenly could again feel the deep presence of God, which made me sensitive to God's "whisper[ing] tenderly to my heart (Hosea 2:14 NIV). Such as, I would hear the Holy Spirit say "I love you with an everlasting heart. (Jeremiah 31:3 NIV) The sweet whispers of the Holy Spirit neutralized every negative thought I had. I became more confident that "If God is for us, who can be against us?" (Romans 8:31 NIV) The times I didn't hear the voice of God; I would cry out in praise. Then I would continue to tell myself "If God gave his dear son for me, he will not turn around and condemn me. He will withhold nothing from me."

The secret to spiritual resolution is fully surrendering and allowing the power of the Holy Spirit to stir your spirit, and the cares of the world will fade away. The power of God changes my actions and his Holy presence stills my heart and soul. Pure worship brings heaven into my situation quickly. I would advise every believer that goes through a season of dryness to continue to trust God's love even when he's silent. Stay in the secret place, pour out your true feelings toward God in prayer, trust, worship, and keep the vision that God has given you. It's impossible for God to lie about his promises for you. (Hebrews 6:18)

CHAPTER 10

Turning Point

The deepest level of worship is praising God regardless of the pain, thanking God during the trials, trusting Him when you're losing hope and loving him when he seems so distant and far away. But, presently, God gave me new wings, and I was flying high above the storms; a deep sense of peace was within me. Never again will I try to carry the weight of the world. I was grateful for the protection and comfort, even when God's presence was hard to find. My worship wasn't based on superficial or pleasant circumstances, but on the understanding that God was to be thanked in both in prosperity and adversity. My gratitude wasn't based on positive thinking, but in a deep and steadfast trust that God was leading and guiding me through all my circumstances. At my lowest point in life, God was my hope, light, strength, and comfort. I was not turning my back on Jesus, I was fighting the good fight of faith.

After praying and worshipping in God's presence, a soft wind hit me. I had a sensation of being intoxicated on his love; I laughed uncontrollably. As tears flooded down my face, all I could do was to dance for joy. Jesus' presence changed everything, I felt light as a feather, with no cares of this world, knowing only the deep peace of the Father. I thought to myself, "What's happening?" I felt as if I was on a deeper spiritual plain. The joy of my salvation was restored; I was experiencing heaven on earth again.

God is the potter and I am the clay, for all my difficult circumstances have molded me to become more like Jesus Christ. I knew that nothing happened out of order, everything I encountered was building me for my future assignment. As I dove deeper into the bible, I received hidden mysteries through the scriptures. This experience made me more aware of my inner light, able to embrace my inner warrior and snatch back my power. Allowing God to love me back to life, and drawing my strength and confidence in the Word of God was the key to maintaining my self-deliverance. I take full responsibility for my story, loving the beauty in my ashes and through that process being courageous and confident enough to be myself. I no longer felt insecurities come into my mind. The more I tapped into the glory of God, there was a switch in my life; God began to turn my burdens into blessings. I no longer dwelt on losing my loved ones, rejection, and negligent treatment from friends. The Lord has been aware of everything that had transpired in my life. In the past, I lived with the illusion that negative events were happening to me, but I now understood that perhaps God allowed rejection for protection. Maybe some of these events occurred to get my attention and to redirect my steps. I trusted that God had the best plan for me. The best plan for me was to surrender to be in the center of God's will and to receive the fullness of the blessings that he had for me.

As I reconnected to my Christ consciousness, the Holy Spirit "Immanuel"(God with us) within me made me bigger than my condition. God can make me become more and do the impossible. Drawing closer to God, I realized that my mind is perfect, with my new-found oneness, which makes me think in alignment with the father, and I can rely on him for all my needs. Inside of me, I felt more confidence, quietness, and security. I just needed to get in a place without distractions, so that I could rest and listen for the Lord's instructions. This new shift caused me to understand the deep mysteries of the Father's heart and divine will for my life. Life was too noisy and there were too many distractions for me to focus and fighting lower spiritual warfare battles, when God wanted me to come higher for a new perspective. In this new dimension, all things are known, my father and I are one; and Christ responds to me when I ask. (Matthew 7:7) I don't need to struggle, worry, or strive; when the time comes the answer will be given to me. That very moment, I let go with confidence, that everything will come to me at the proper time. As long as I align myself with the living word and connect in faith with the precious name of our Lord Jesus Christ, then all things will be possible. Yes! And amen. (2 Corinthians 1:20) For it is when we have the power of expectancy and faith towards a particular situation that we see full manifestations of miracles.

The more I worshipped, the more God poured his glory on me. I learned that there could never be any negative circumstances from the mind of God, and that very day, the Lord gave me a makeover. I was assured that my confidence would never be in my own abilities, but the supernatural power of Christ that had perfected me into his image. I relied on Christ's power to create my own reality. My world was manifested by my thoughts and convictions. In my friends, I saw nothing but cooperation and assistance. I refused to acknowledge disunity and only saw positivity. I had sympathy, empathy, and compassion for all things and all people. I didn't order things to be made in my time, but trusted God to show me the time, need, and the location. Each moment and day brought my life closer to the realization of success, harmony, and peace. All of life happened in my heart and mind, and I wanted to focus only on goodness, love, and expansion.

Our life is a product of our thoughts. Every good thing that came my way was mine to claim and therefore, confirmed my faith, by demonstrating the living word, which becomes physical reality. From the beginning of Genesis 1:3, God spoke the world into existence. We are a reflection of our heavenly father, so we can call things that are not as if they are. This means you can prophesy to your current situation and speak life into your circumstance, For it is written, ". . . let the weak say, I *am* strong." (Joel 3:10 NIV) Changes will occur as long as they abide in the Word of God. I believed in my heart, so it would be done. Awaking to the voice of our heart is necessary to hear revelations from God, for we are one with all people, life, and all things. Limitations are but an illusion; where I am weak, I am strong in the Holy Spirit. Don't let any perceived lack weaken your faith. Instead let us tap into the unlimited dunamis power from the Lord. For it is written, "Now unto him that is able to do exceeding abundantly above all that we ask or think, according to the power that worketh in us" (Ephesians 3:20 KJV) The secret is that our thoughts impact what we manifest.

God is perfect, there can be no obstacles or problems in the mind of God. In fact, I learned both evil forces and good forces can play a role to bring goodness out of life. A great example would be Joseph's story when he says, "You intended to harm me, but God intended it for good to accomplish what is now being done, the saving of many lives". (Genesis 50:20 NIV) In this passage, we learn that God can bring good from evil for those who trust in him. Be patient and endure hardships with confidence. Do you trust God enough to wait patiently for him to bring good out of a bad situation? Christians must trust God. Think about it: If God governs the universe to bring day into night, then I'm confident that he can turn my burdens into blessings. All I have to do is to keep hope alive, so that God will work miraculous power in and through me.

Like Joseph, I had to endure long-suffering. There was no need for me to stress, in the strength of my believe my faith will make my dreams come to pass. I constantly reminded myself, The Holy Spirit is living in me and is around me, and I could depend on him for everything. Everything is connected, and I began to see the illusion of obstacles in my way. I refused to accept the negative, and I was creating positive things with my thoughts. Whatever I gave focus to, I gave strength to; the mind is very powerful. Your mind can make you a prisoner or as free as you choose.

Based on my experience, whatever I believed and accepted was created in my life. I had great faith, but I was still a human being, with human concerns. At times, my eyes and five senses became confused with problems; I would then immediately turn away and focus on the abundance, love, protection, and goodness of the Lord. I learned how to master my mind and emotions by reprogramming my mind to picture what I wanted to see; it certainly came to pass. Error was the result of isolating myself or experiencing disconnection from the spiritual presence of Jesus Christ. As a Christian, I had to be able to quiet my ego from worldly troubles and meditate on the Word of God; this is the only way I gained wisdom, knowledge, power, self awareness, and supernatural strength. God was constantly creating what I thought, and the light of the law was bigger than me. I held my thoughts on good things, relaxing and focusing on the positive. Things were changing for me drastically. I knew that Jesus was more than enough for me.

Regardless of what challenges you face in life, keep your mind steadfastly focused on the good. For it is written, "Finally, brothers and sisters, whatever is true, whatever is noble, whatever is right, whatever is pure, whatever is lovely, whatever is admirable--if anything is excellent or praiseworthy--think about such things." (Philippians 4:8 NIV) When I focused on what I desired, I was able to achieve it and manifest it in my life by faith. For it was the strength of my belief in God's word, that my faith would make it so. Things slowly but surely more pieces of the puzzle appeared, and everything started to come together for me.

Solitude allowed me to go deep within my spirit. When I began to feel frustration, sadness, or discouragement, I often encouraged myself by reading positive biblical stories. It was my spirit man that governed my whole life. I knew that I was more than my body, my thoughts, my life experience-- that I was a spirit-being in living in a body. I acknowledged my thoughts and I had the power to either accept or reject.

God heals your inner soul when you take captivity over any negative thoughts. God is there with you, waiting for your words to change, so he can manifest his wonderful plans for your life. As scripture says, "As a Man Thinketh in His Heart so is He" (Proverbs 23:7 KJV) Whatever I chose to think about was mine, and whatever I rejected would never touch me. From heart to head, the Lord had taken me on a new and deeper journey. I felt an intimate bond between me and my loving Heavenly Father; I was open to the leading of the Holy Spirit. Hallelujah, the right ideas were provided to me. I removed all barriers and replaced them with God's purpose for me. Wisdom and understanding was given to me about my current situation and the power of my mind brought spiritual blessings into my world. I had insights and new understandings of how to fix my problems. I knew that everything comes from the heart to the Christ consciousness, then the mind. It is the Holy Spirit that communicates through the heart. The heart empowers us to take action. All wisdom and knowledge flows from the heart to the head and, finally to the body. For it is written, "Above all else, guard your heart, for everything you do flows from it." (Proverbs 4:23 NIV) It's important to guard the heart, because if we have a sick heart, we can block the Holy Spirit. Our hearts operate out of love and desire, which dictates, to a great extent, on how we live and how we commune with the Holy Spirit.

When I walk in the spirit, I stand in the love, peace, and joy of God. Nothing evil can get to me with my mind steadfast on the Lord. If I get into doubt, fear, or anger, I am pulled out of the glory realm. When I worship God, I excite heaven and create a doorway for my angelic access to the Heavenly Realm. When we enter the Holy of Holies, all revelation becomes known. It is vital that all believers enter his gates with praise and thanksgiving; (Psalm 100:4) and continually be filled by the spirit of God. Only God alone is worthy to be worshiped. What is your attitude towards God? Do you willingly and joyfully come into God's presence, or do you go through the motions, reluctantly going to church? God inhabits the praises of his people. (Psalm 22:3) We show love for the creator when we constantly have an attitude of gratitude. My hope and trust remained in God as I reminisced on the past victories I've experienced with God. I felt a deep peace as I rested under the shadow of his wings.

Worship is the most powerful and effective way to get God on the scene. "God *is* Spirit, and those who worship Him must worship in spirit and truth."(John 4:24 NIV) When we worship, we get ourselves off of the throne and put God on the throne. The Apostle Paul gives us a wonderful example of how great worship can make things happen. When Paul and Silas began to sing songs and praise God, the chains fell off when heaven intervened in their situation and they were freed from prison. (Acts 16:24-26) Do you ever feel that you're in a hopeless situation? Try praising God until the sun comes out again. When we're in a situation, God is looking for our faith, when we activate our faith, then all things are possible in our lives.

My advice for other believers who desire to become intoxicated by God's love is to press closer to God at all times. If the storm never stops, dance in it knowing that God is faithful to complete what he starting concerning your life. (Philippians 1:6). Do you often feel as if you're not making progress in your spiritual growth? Trust in the word of God, praise God instead of problems because it's impossible for God to lie. Faithfully serving others and keeping a heart of thanksgiving in a difficult time honors the Lord. My personal experience of capturing the heart of God is when I fixed my eyes on Jesus. There I felt a deep peace. (Philippians 4:7) Jesus emphasized the importance of loving God wholeheartedly when he quoted the first commandment "Love the Lord your God with all your heart and with all your soul and with all your strength and with all your mind." (Luke 10:27 NIV) The heart and praise must marry. You must involve the mind, will, and emotions in your praise. Sing your heart out to the Lord, for he is worthy. We don't sing a song just because it has a nice beat or smooth melody; it must be fully directed to the Lord. It's vital to understand what the song means, so you can sing it with all your heart. I intertwine praise with thanksgiving while I intertwine worship with surrender. God's peace differs from the world's peace. (John 14:27) True peace is not quoting positive affirmations for positive thinking. It comes from knowing that God is in control and relying only on him. All born-again Christian citizenship in Christ's Kingdom is sure, our destiny set, and we win all demonic battles on the Cross. Therefore, all believers can let God's peace guard their heart against anxiety.

I would have never made it without God; I love to worship him. God is not a physical being limited to one place. The precious Holy Spirit is present everywhere, and he can be worshiped anywhere. I'm feeling a shift in the atmosphere, I was starting to feel so alive!

CHAPTER 11

Jesus is Alive

Often people confuse God as the universe of energy, but in actuality, the Holy Spirit is a person who lives inside every born-again Christian. It's Christ Jesus dwelling in my heart is the Hope of Glory, also known as Immanuel "God with us". (Matthew 1:23 NIV) The Bible proves this in 1 John 4:4 KJV: "Greater is he that lives in me than in the world." Jesus conquered all evil and his word lives in our hearts! Many times when I get into worship, I feel the Holy Spirit moving under my skin and a sensation tingling in my fingers. It is only when I am in complete quietness, that Jesus would speak revelations to me through dreams, biblical scriptures, or open visions. Born-again Christians are glory-carriers of Heaven, for the Holy Spirit watches over us and protect us.

In order to connect to the deepest, innermost parts of the heart of God and to tap into His peace you have to have solitude and quietness. Meditating on the word of God with no distractions is the price you have to pay to encounter the fullness of God's spirit, which is the seven spirits of the Lord. (Isaiah 11:2-3) Meditation is visitation with God. Separation from the world is necessary to elevate your mind. It can be lonely at the top. As a minister, educated in the Word, I've been a living witness for thousands of followers, yet my human connections may not be fulfilling. For believers, loneliness could only exist if one has no sense of purpose or connection with Jesus. For full divine access, I had to quiet the mind and let the spirit speak from within, for focus and sensitivity to the Holy Spirit, and to tune into that spiritual frequency. What does that look like? How does it feel? Some people feel a tingling in the body, other people feel a heat sensation in their heart, and still others may laugh uncontrollably. As for me, I felt light as a feather, like I could fly. When I became very quiet, I gained deep awareness, which helped me have the conscious state of Christ. Meditating on the Word of God led to the words on the page coming alive for me. For example, I could picture the Gospel scene of Peter walking on water, I could actually picture the emotions of Jesus's love and Peter's doubt as the story played out. (Matthew 14:30) Deep meditation opened my eyes to the meaning of the words.

As I drew deeper into the spirit, I enjoyed my intimate moments with my Father God, and I no longer valued anything in the world. There are some times when I don't have the strength to work, but the Holy Spirit wakes me up and strengthens me to do his will. Jesus constantly encourages me; I never fear to be alone or have a loss of direction. For Roman 8:14 NIV, states ". . . that all who are being led by the Spirit of God, these are the sons of God". The King of the Universe is fellowshipping with me. What a privilege! In his presence, there is the fullness of joy and peace.

Only Jesus can give you peace that lasts. Immanuel (God with us) dwells in us and is alive! The Holy Spirit is God's seal that we belong to him and his deposit guaranteeing that he will do what he has promised. The Holy Spirit is like a down payment, a deposit, a validating signature on the contract. The presence of the Holy Spirit in us demonstrates the genuineness of our faith, probes that we are God's children, and secret eternal life for us. His power works in us to transform us now, and what we experience now is a taste of the total change we will experience in eternity. Child of God—Persevere in the good, keep a pure heart, keep standing for what is right, and you will overcome and prevail in the end.

Jesus Christ is alive, and he constantly walks with me to order my steps with the daily revelation on how I can continuously live in his peace and freedom. The Lord showed me the importance of praying according to seasons, time, and purpose, as stated in the well-known verses from Ecclesiastes, which, in part, says, "It's a time to search and a time to give up; a time to keep and a time to throw away." (Ecclesiastes 3:6 NIV) I felt a sense of peace when I gained an understanding as to the season and prayed accordingly. My simple steps to enter God's rest was to discover, accept, and appreciate God's perfect timing. Although it's difficult to be patient during a crisis, it's important to trust and obey God in every circumstance. Moving ahead of God's timing is disobedience and rebellion against God's instructions. Even though I desperately prayed for God to stop the trials, I had to follow God's instructions and persevere like a champion. Longsuffering means being patient with a situation or person, even if you are hurting, while always trusting in God's deliverance.The scriptures comforted me (Psalm 119:76) and gave me the confidence to know that God is with me fighting all my battles. (Romans 8:31)

Our Lord Jesus Christ is faithful. He will stay by our side even when we have endured so much that we seem to have no hope left. (Philippians 1:6) We may be faithless at times, but Jesus is faithful to his promises to be with us "to the very end of the age"(Matthew 28:20 NIV) Don't refuse Christ's help, for he is the only hope for humanity. In the midst of dangerous persecutions, stand firm in the faith. When we are presented with challenges, we are being tested, where God sifts through to distinguish between superficiality or true commitment. When you are pressured to give up or turn your back on Christ, don't do it!. Remember, God is aware of your circumstances; don't forsake your eternal reward because of the intensity of today's pain. Remain faithful, knowing that your weakness will present an opportunity for Christ to strengthen you. Knowing that we will live forever with God in a place without sin and suffering can help us live above the pain that we face in this life.

Life is a daily faith fight, but I have the confidence to know that I serve a God of all possibilities. As an intercessor, it was my duty to pray against the devil's schemes and pray that I too manifest God's will in people's lives. Often I've seen myself praying for people, giving advice, and witnessing their breakthroughs, yet my dreams were postponed. This reminds me of the biblical story in Genesis 41, where Joseph was translating dreams to Pharaoh while they postponed his dreams. I continued to serve God and stand with selfless faith. The more I spoke the word with faith, the more I experienced a change in my world. The only way to fight the fierce spiritual battle I was facing was to continue to eat my spiritual food, which was the Word of God. I echoed Jeremiah who said, "Your words were found, and I ate them, and your words became to me a joy and delight of my heart." (Jeremiah 15:16). This was the exact case for me, the power of God's word restored me. It completely transformed me in spending time with Jesus — sitting with him, lamenting to him, seeking counsel, and listening to his leading from the Holy Spirit. That is exactly what I've received, for the resurrection king is forever living inside of me. Never break faith, Jesus is alive.

CHAPTER 12

Resurrection Power

After being buried deep underground and overwhelmed with a barrage of emotions; I was in despair.

In transition, I felt alone and separated from everything I had known and in emotional pain from being rejected, mocked, and isolated. I was thinking to myself, "Who can I trust?" I had to encourage myself in the Lord, like David did when his enemies talked about stoning him. (1 Samuel 30:6) Faced with my tragedy of losing my family members, my friends, and my dreams I had to find supernatural strength in the Lord, instead of blaming others and falling into defeat and victimhood. I have always taken responsibility for my circumstances, and I would find a way to fulfill my destiny.

I realized I was the seed of heaven and God would pour out rain to allow me to flourish again. Typically, Seed placed in the ground doesn't grow unless it dies first. Jesus said it best: "Very truly I tell you, unless a kernel of wheat falls to the ground and dies, it remains only a single seed. But if it dies, it produces many seeds." (John 12:24 NIV) This parable paints a picture and foreshadowing of the price that Jesus paid for our redemption, and shows how resurrection works, not just literally, but figuratively, too. Each time we die spiritually, we rise again, equipped with more knowledge and wisdom. As Christians, we must die daily to

---

ourselves and learn to love like Jesus. I actually gathered strength from my pain, and I used it positively to help others.

When I look back at that spiritual death, I can see that God's heart was reaching out to me in love and comfort, as Paul writes, "He comforts us in all our troubles so that we can comfort others. When they are troubled, we will be able to give them the same comfort God has given us." (2 Corinthians 1:4 NIV) I felt like I was in a spiritual coma; I didn't act like my normal self. There was a time where depression was so deep I asked God to take me up to Heaven. I was ready for the rapture! But, unfortunately, that wasn't going to happen any time soon. But I did lean on the Psalms to comfort me, and I prayed from Psalm 143:4-7 NIV, "I sat there in despair, my spirit draining away, my heart heavy, like lead. I remembered the old days, went over all you've done, pondered the ways you've worked, Stretched out my hands to you, as thirsty for you as a desert thirsty for rain. Hurry with your answer, God! I'm nearly at the end of my rope. Don't turn away; don't ignore me! That would be certain death." Have you ever felt that no one cares what is happening to you? I understood how David felt when he wrote those words, I had to cry out in agonizing tears; laid out prostrate before the Lord. I was pouring out my inner feelings to God because I was losing hope, paralyzed with fear and had fallen into a very deep depression. Then, began to reminisce about the Lord's work in my life. Still, I no longer had a passion or motivation for living or fulfilling my dreams. I was emotionally and spiritually depleted. Help! I called out to God, but no answer came, at least not as I expected.

Similar to Lazarus' experience in John 11:6 NIV, which tells us, "When therefore he heard that he was sick, he stayed for four days in the place where he was." Many may find it strange that God would delay helping such an urgent case, yet a four-day delay served the purpose of increasing the people's need to rely on God's help. Jesus rose on the third day. Perhaps Jesus wanted to give Lazarus' family a greater gift of waiting for their brother to die so that God could resurrect him again. In my situation, God's purpose was to bring glory to himself in my life but never to leave me separated from his love for me. Often, it is difficult to see God's perspective during trials, because God specializes in bringing good out of any bad situation.

Nothing is too hard for God to resurrect, as we saw in the story of Lazarus being raised from death by Jesus Christ back to life. (John 11) This was an amazing illustration of how Jesus has power over life and death. Recalling back to John 11:4, Jesus knew that his best friend would die, yet he told his disciples that his death was not final. This was an opportunity for God to display the mighty power and glory of his resurrection. If Lazarus was raised back to life after his four days of burial, I was confident that Jesus would revive me and bring my dreams back to life. I knew that there would always hope for me. As a born-again, spirit-filled Christian, although I allowed darkness to enter my life through depression over what I lost in life, I kept praying and renewing my mind in scripture, so I didn't fall for Satan's lies. Believers should never evaluate their life based on current conditions because God's promises are forever. We have a wonderful future in Christ, as long as we stay faithful to the end. Who are we to question God? No matter our situation, we should never lose faith in our Lord and Savior, speaking the word over your life can change any situation. I can definitely testify to Luke 1:37 NIV, "No word of God will ever fail".

Some Christians believe that if they have been saved or born-again it protects them from wickedness in the world. Satan loves such spiritual blindness and false beliefs. Temptation and persecution will always be there, yet by submitting to God, Christians can avoid giving Satan access to enter. Sin, pain, and suffering will always exist in the world. It is written, "The righteous person may have many troubles, but the LORD delivers him from them all; (Psalm 34:19 NIV). Daily, we fight spiritual warfare, Christians overcome attacks by abiding in the promises of God. If we ignore the word of God, it will destroy us. (Hosea 4:6)

During my life trials, I spoke the word of God over my life and it resurrected me back to life. Praise the living God for being faithful to keeping his promises as given in the holy bible. If God brought life to my dead places, he would definitely use me to bring life to the spiritual dead conditions in other people lives. As Christians, we must always take responsibility and be accountable for our life. I would advise all non-believers to receive choose life in Christ, Jesus will save you from Sin, Satan, and Self. Naturally, every human is born in a carnal and sinful state, but Christ is the only good thing in us because we learn how to crucify our selfish desires and practice selfless living in the spirit. He will fill you up with his Holy Spirit and empower you to walk in righteousness and dunamis power. As I discussed in the paragraph above, no Christian is safe from evil. Salvation and baptism does not shield believers from dark forces, which is one of Satan's biggest deceptions. Life is constant spiritual warfare and battlefield of the mind; therefore, it's important to know the Word of God to overcome evil with good. A great example would be Apostle Paul experienced many struggles. In Romans chapter 6 & 7 Paul talks about his fight against sin, "I do what I hate" (Rom 7:15 NIV), "evil is present in me" (Rom 7:21 NIV) and says "Oh wretched Man I Am" (Rom 7:24-25 KJV). In Chapter 8, He admits he can do nothing and needs the Holy Spirit constantly. Likewise, I realized that the only thing that is valuable and good in me in is Christ Jesus, for it is the power of the Holy Spirit that makes me walk holy and upright.

I am often guilty of seeing the immediate suffering of physical circumstances and I forget that God has bigger things in mind for my life. "For I know the plans I have for you," declares the LORD, "plans to prosper you and not to harm you, plans to give you hope and a future" (Jeremiah 29:11 NIV). I've never doubted God plans for my life, yet I constantly prayed for God to take the pain and suffering from me. I learned to be patient and trust that God is answering my prayers during silence. For there is greater glory on the other side of difficult times, I remain confident of this: I will see the goodness of the LORD in the land of the living. (Psalm 27:13) Even in my darkness, I still had a ray of hope. As I reminisce about God's faithfulness in my life I am reminded: Thank you for being my physician, protector, provider, counselor, defender, entertainer, wisdom, strength, joy, peace, refuge, and my bridegroom. Jesus, I love you forever. I will never forget who you are and what you have done for me. You never fail, when I look at you. You're my breath, life, everything! Never underestimate God's mighty power and unconditional love. For the Lord is faithful and mighty in his deeds.

For it was the living word spoken over the life that sustained me. I had to learn how to be patient in my difficulties without being anxious or taking matters into my own hands. I had to rely on John 11:25 NIV," Jesus said to her, " I am the resurrection and the life. The one who believes in me will live, even though they die". It is impossible for God to lie daily I mediated on this scripture. I put my hope in this word because I believed in Christ, that he will awaken my spiritual life again, death cannot conquer or diminish. When a born-again Christian is sealed by the Holy Spirit, nothing can break that seal. (Ephesians 1:13-14)

During my transformation as a born-again Christian I gave God ownership and access to my life; I can not predict what he will do with my life. I had to learn to trust that all would be for his glory, even the spiritual death I encountered. God had called me to be a disciple, so I knew that he would restore me to wholeness and give me new life, resurrecting me with anointing and fresh fire of the Holy Spirit. Like a "diamond in the rough," I was refined from a piece of coal, after facing all kinds of pressure, God turned me into a diamond.

Because I died with Christ, I got to live again and rise with Christ. Because of Jesus Christ's resurrection we have hope for the future. I am marked and chosen, therefore I must model Christ by identifying with the sufferings of Jesus. This was my reason to praise God Almighty every day because I fought the good fight of faith; I did not quit.

With the power of the Holy Spirit, I had defeated death. I felt like my hope and dreams were alive again. God healed me mentally, spiritually, and physically. God always has the final word on all things in heaven and earth. Usually, there is a correlation between God's word with faith and the action we take to manifest positive outcomes. With that being said, as long as I kept my faith in God it would be impossible for me to fail. Things were coming together, I was feeling liberated, and a creativity bloomed with pursuing my passion again. It was so incredible to know that I was under the watchful eyes of God and He was providing for my every need. It blessed me to experience deeper intimacy with God; he had resurrected my physical, mental, and spiritual life again. Convinced that I was under the watchful eyes of God, I came to know that nothing that God has his hand on can fail, and that includes you and me. Speaking the Word over my life is the reason I am still alive today. Even though I felt like I was in deep spiritual death, faith allowed me to be resurrected again.

Chapter 13

Unshakable

As I grew more into a deeper relationship with God, I felt a burning passion in my heart to boldly spread the undiluted word of God. It felt like a charge up in my spirit to speak the word uncompromising and unapologetically. Perhaps my past trials have equipped me to face opposition with courage on my new assignment. I would never compromise to popular culture or traditionalists; this was the reason I experienced rejection in the past. However, the adversity has pushed me into the greater anointing. Instead of being frustrated by my failures, I have fueled my righteous anger to overcome every limitation based on God's promises for my life. Remember, "We don't wrestle against flesh and blood, but against principalities, against powers, against the rulers of the darkness of this world, against spiritual wickedness in high places." (Ephesians 6:12 NIV). The moment a Christian is a born-again, automatically they are a threat to the kingdom of darkness. Life is a constant battle of the mind; Christian growth is like a strenuous race or fight. I'm prepared to take this new journey, headed to the Big Apple. That's right, New York City.

I needed to leave my hometown, where people were so familiar with me, so God instructed me to go to New York. I packed all my belongings and drove approximately 25 hours from Texas to New York City. This was a huge faith move because I didn't have many resources and I knew no one in New York City.

After living in a hotel, my resources were depleted. I had so many ideas, and not enough money to accomplish my vision. Greatness comes at a price, and I refused to settle for less. I had to sacrifice my comfort to fulfill God's plan for my life. The entire process was humbling, but this dependence on God had grown my faith in incalculable ways. I continued to trust that God would make a way for me. I have to admit, I found myself homeless for a couple of days, before I was able to secure an apartment. Although it was demeaning, I slept in my car, while still parked in the hotel lot. Hoping that no one would see me, I would put up window blinds; as if I was protecting the window from the sun. Determined to fulfill my dreams, I set a temporary plan in place until I found an available and suitable place to live. During the day, I would work evangelizing on the streets, in the afternoons I would bathe at the gym, and during the evening, rest in my car. This was the price I had to pay. I kept on encouraging myself by meditating on Roman 8:28 NIV, "All things work together for good to them that love God, to those who are called according to his purpose". Even though I didn't know how or where my next meal or home would be; I continually trusted God.Eventually, God would bless me with a new town home in my new location, but my priority was time to build a church in New York City and preach the good news of Jesus Christ.

Speaking the word of God is dangerous work. I can recall an incident, evangelizing the word of God when a person sitting nearby began arguing against the words I was speaking, grabbed a bottle of beer, and threw it down and smashed it by my feet. Although I was wearing sandals, by God's grace, the broken glass didn't cut my foot, and I only had small scratches. God's protection for me was limitless, and I was shaken up, but not physically harmed. Perhaps, my attacker felt her beliefs were being threatened and that spiritual backlash came because the Lord was using me to convert a non-believer to the gospel. Immediately, I looked at the one who threw the bottle and boldly stood up; rebuked the argumentative spirit that was opposing me, and instantly, she submitted under the authority of Jesus and backed off.

For it is written, "I have given you authority to trample on snakes and scorpions and to overcome all the power of the enemy; nothing will harm you" (Luke 10:19 NIV). I fought back by speaking directly to the unclean spirit, for God had given me, as a Christian, power and authority over every spirit that would oppose the word. As I see God's wonders at work in and through me, I never lose sight of the greatest wonder of all, which is my heavenly citizenship.

Some may question, "Are we always supposed to be loving towards others?" Yes, but we never tolerate sin. Tolerating sin will allow Satan to cause destruction and temptation in one's life. We can't be friends with sin and expect our lives to remain unaffected. As believers grow deeper in the things of God... sin, injustice, and suffering in the world may cause holy anger. To read more about the scripture of holy anger, read Exodus 32:4 or John 2:13-17.

Based on my experience, frustration has pushed me into greater anointing. Some of my trials caused me to experience righteous anger and I was able to use it in positive ways to become victorious in my life. For example, when people told me that I would never amount to anything, I began to arise above my situation. Holy anger should make a person handle an *action*, never a person. I would begin to pray for solutions in intensive yet aggressive prayer with the Lord. For it is written, " From the days of John the Baptist until now, the kingdom of heaven has been subjected to violence and violent people have been raiding it." (Matthew 11:12 NIV) Prayer changes everything. I also used righteous anger to overcome anxiety or fear. I commanded over my life that I was able to do all things with Christ Jesus on my side. (Philippians 4:13) Believers should witness with strength, move mountains with faith, and overcome with love.

Never compromise with sin, always stand strong and fight in the power of our Lord Jesus Christ. It is better to stand with God judging the world, than standing with the world being judged against God. All believers have a common goal, and that is to positively affect others with the good news of the gospel. We dim our light as believers when we are quiet when we should speak up, compromising with the crowd, denying Christ, tolerating sin, and ignoring the needs of others.

How should a believer handle life's trials when assuming a posture of faith? The secret to overcoming trials is putting on the whole armor of God, ". . . that ye may stand against the wiles of the devil." (Ephesians 6:11-18 KJV) To withstand and overcome attacks we must depend on God's strength and use every piece of our spiritual armor. Often disciples face powerful unseen spiritual forces whose goal is to defeat Christ's church. The moment we become Christian, automatically we become a threat to Satan's kingdom. Then the kingdom of darkness' goal is to entice believers to turn away from Christ and back to sin. Although we are assured victory with Jesus, we must engage in the struggle of spiritual warfare. Christians must use supernatural power the Holy Spirit has provided that to defeat Satan.

Allow me to simplify what it means to put on the full armor of God as a new follower. First, we must wear the belt of the armor of truth. Satan tries to fill our minds with lies, and sometimes his lies sound like the truth. The only solution is to speak God's truth, which can defeat Satan's lies. Second, wearing the breastplate of righteousness will defeat Satan's schemes. Often the enemy attacks our heart with hurts, this is the seat of our emotions, self-worth, and trust. God's righteousness is the breastplate that protects our heart and ensures his approval. The Father approves of us because he loves us and sent his Son to die for us. We must always meditate on scriptures that would boost our self-esteem. The next device is our footgear which is our peace. Christians must have the readiness to spread the good news. Satan wants us to think telling others the good news is a worthless and hopeless task. The enemy wants Christians to believe that the task is too big and the negative responses are too much to handle. But the footgear God gives us is the motivation to continue to proclaim the true peace available in God, news that the world needs to hear. Next, the shield of faith will protect us from the darts of the enemy. Satan attacks us in the form of insults, setbacks, and temptations. But the shield of faith protects us from Satan flaming arrows. The word of God gives us the patience to endure trials. With God perspective, we can see beyond our circumstances and know that Jesus Christ has given us the victory. Next, the helmet of Salvation is to guard our mind. Satan wants us to doubt God, and that Jesus Christ is our salvation. The helmet protects our mind from doubting God's saving work for us. Last, the word of God is an offensive weapon. When we are tempted, we need to trust in the word of God.

I advise all new believers to never let your faith be shaken, trust in God's word. Pray, there is power in the name of Jesus. Everything happens for a reason. God is directing all of our steps. Wherever there is a lack in your life, call on Jesus to restore you. Encourage yourself, keep trusting and praising God. For non-believers, a life without Christ is a life without hope or purpose. Surrender your life to Jesus and allow the Holy Spirit to lead and direct your life.

CHAPTER 14

Steady Building

All things were coming together beautifully for me, and I was living in a beautiful townhome, in a nice neighborhood and all my basic needs were met. I thanked God for my beautiful townhome, yet I was depending on Him to provide a building for my ministry. Everyday I prayed for additional resources to be able to rent a space for my church and I hoped to find a spacious place. Even though I had accumulated more expenses, I knew that with faith and focus would make my dreams come into existence. I was determined to make something out of nothing. I began to set up events outdoors, so I applied for the park permits having programs outdoors. I purchased a portable speaker, a microphone, and a tent, but with so many expenses, my current budget was threatening to stop me from fulfilling my destiny. I will do whatever it took for me to succeed. The Bible tells us, "Do not despise these small beginnings, for the Lord rejoices to see the work begin..." (Zechariah 4:10 NIV) It was easy for me to reminisce everything I lost in the past. In fact, sometimes I was disheartened when I realized that I have downgraded my life tremendously. I echo Job, " The Lord gave and the Lord has taken away; may the name of the Lord be praised."(Job 1:21 NIV) It took me some time to get over losing loved ones, homes, businesses, and my dreams; but admitting my grief allowed me to recognize and overcome my past failures. Even though the new church would not match the size and splendor of the previous churches, I've built in the past, I trust that God will never fail me. It took a while, but with the Lord help, I could bury my past. I believe that if I remain faithful in the small opportunities and continue to do what is right, just, and fair; then I please my God. I began where I was and made the best out of every situation, leaving all the final results to God.

Failure was never an option for me. Day by day, this is how I proceeded:

Day 1: The Lord blessed me with a few workers to start, but in time I knew we would grow by the special grace of God. I put all my resources of knowledge, experience, and organization into determining what we should do. Remnants of the pain from the tragic event that occurred from my past failures, introduced feelings of uncertainty, but all I could do was pray and focus on God's mission for my life. I had a brand new team that was supporting me on this new assignment, yet I still had to train them for the ministry. I could move beyond grief to a specific action that would help people. I fasted and prayed for several days, including praise, thanksgiving, and rededication of my commitment to God. By the end of my prayer time, I knew what actions to take. My difficult decision turned into proper perspective and actions. Godly ambition stirred up in my spirit, and I was confident that God would fulfill all promises concerning my life. It's by faith, work, and the grace of God that we achieve blessings or success effortlessly, unlike worldly ambition, which focuses on selfish gain and egotistic matters. However, Godly ambition focused on looking out for others and to serve God. I wanted more than anything else, to please God and do his will.

Day 2: I prayed for success with this new assignment, not just for the strength to cope with these problems. Yet the success I prayed about was not for personal advantage or position, my goal was to build a church that would teach the good salvation news and uplift, strengthen, and heal people that are experiencing any difficulties in life. Every time I would reach progress or success in an area of the ministry, setbacks would break out among my team. Experience gave me the wisdom to resolve the matter, and I knew that these delays were a sign that huge blessings were coming. Nothing good comes easy, and I had to constantly gird myself against spiritual warfare. It is the devil job to kill, steal, and destroy good things in life, especially when feeling threatened. (John 10:10) As the distractions and spiritual attacks continue to breakout, I continued to pray at all times, even when talking with others. I knew that God is always in charge, and he would never give me more than I can handle. I trusted that God love for me would defend me as I continue to build the church legacy. The Lord grant me the position, power, and many good organizational skills, but I still acknowledged that I depended on God's gracious hand and power over my life. Without God's wisdom and strength, my efforts would be in vain. Every day, I took a moment to acknowledge God's miraculous power operating over my life.

Day 3: When I arrived at the park, I faced huge opposition. People were watching our every move and complaining about loud worship music. Once I started speaking, increasingly people became curious and interested to hear what I had to say, and joined the service. After the prayer service, people were sharing much testimony; however, the warfare increased as well. My directional signs were knocked down and I assumed that the wind had blown them over but, looking closer, I saw that someone destroyed the church signs with spray paint and knocked down the church stands. Opposition typically comes with the territory, therefore I needed to increase security in the protocol department. To guard against oppression and attacks, we must keep our minds steadfast on God for perfect peace. For it is written, "You will keep in perfect peace those whose minds are steadfast because they trust in you." (Isaiah 26:3 NIV) We can never avoid strife in the world, but with God, we can now perfect peace even in turmoil. Anytime we are devoted to him, our whole attitude is steady and stable. I laugh at the attacks because the chaos in the world would never shake my devotion to God and his unchanging love and mighty power. I continue to pray in my heart and work hard for the Lord. Eventually, my hard work will pay off and people would have a church to attend to receive a solution for the problems. If you're going through ongoing problems, keep your thoughts focused and trust in God.

Victory belonged to us. I was confident that with God behind my project, I would not allow spiritual attacks or threats to stop me. While building my congregation, daily, I had an evangelism team going out to spread the Good New of Salvation. Every person we met was an opportunity for the ministry of evangelism. The mission field was all around us, all we had to do was constantly pray for more workers to help fulfill God's will. For it is written, "The harvest is plentiful, but the laborers are few." (Luke 10:2 NIV) Jesus encouraged the disciples not just to do the work but also to pray for workers. I was very aware that a part of every missionary's job is to pray for new workers to help newcomers learn the ministry functions. Believers were not to work alone most of the time, for God wants them to pray, recruit, and equip others to join them as they explore opportunities to serve Jesus and others.

Day 4: Still steadily climbing to success. Daily, God had given me the strength to endure both direct and indirect pressures and the wisdom to see through any obstacles. Where would I be without the grace of God? Sensitive to the Holy Spirit, I didn't want to miss out on the appointed time. Remaining focused and making the best of each day that was given to me, I didn't want to move too fast nor too slow. I just wanted to seek God's guidance, instead of rushing ahead with my agenda, which would have caused more problems. When a new situation arose, I made it a habit to inquire about the Lord's wisdom and guidance. The lessons of the past have taught me the importance of operating on God's timing and not mine. I could have saved myself a lot of trouble by remaining patient on my appointed timing. It wasn't easy to rebuild a whole church congregation, yet with the power of The Holy Spirit, I could delegate the prophetic strategies to fulfill heaven's mandate.

Day 5: With my outdoor revival, I felt good about using the limited resources I had; however, I didn't want to underestimate the power of God to provide beyond my wildest dreams. As Paul writes, "Now to him who is able to do immeasurably more than all we ask or imagine, according to his power is at work within us..." (Ephesians 3:20 NIV) I thought to myself," God is able to give me favor with the financial institution to get funding for building a church in New York." After receiving divine directions for the ministry, I still wasn't sure how everything would come to pass. For the dream was bigger than me, yet I trusted that this would be an opportunity for God to show off his miraculous powers. Whether indoors or outdoors, my goal was to give God my best in the kingdom work. Often the faith walk is both exciting and scary because God only gives us pieces of the puzzle. If God would have shown us everything in store for us, then we wouldn't need to depend on or have faith in Jesus. Still walking courageously, I trusted that God will unfold more of his mystery concerning my life as I continued to walk on that narrow path. I had no fear because I knew that God would order my steps. (Psalm 37:23) I delighted in doing God will for my life, therefore, I had the confidence to know protection and provision would be my portion as long if I was obedient. After carefully planning and completing the project, then we could go public with this mission. I shared my vision with enthusiasm, inspiring my team to work hard to achieve God's assignment. I knew it was a dream from God, because it felt nearly impossible to achieve, but with faith all things are possible. (Matthew 19:26)

As we planned events and set up the stage for the revival, some of the workers grew weary and complained about the work being too hard, yet with my gentle encouragement we were able to complete our work. External forces, like rainy weather, transportation needs, and permit problems did come to try to delay our project. Occasionally, I thought about relocating my ministry. Yet, I had invested too much. I couldn't allow anyone or anything to make me feel stressed or discouraged on this assignment.

Although I was not going to be hindered, anytime someone stands for goodness and truth, there will always be resistance and ridicule. Referring to Nehemiah 4:1-5 NIV, "... He ridiculed the Jews. . Will they restore their wall? Will they offer sacrifices? Will they finish in a day? . . . Hear us, our God, for we are despised." In this scripture, Sanballat and Tobiah (the ones criticizing the Jews) were causing trouble and ridiculing which caused discouragement and despair. Their goal was to dissuade the Jews from building the wall. However, Nehemiah did not focus on distractions from the people, but he prayed and continued to focus on rebuilding the wall. I personally can relate to this situation, I have been lied to, mocked, and criticized about my faith. It felt as if every time I was making progress with the ministry, massive attacks would take place. I had to remain focused on my vision while praying and singing in my heart when I was opposed by people. Deep inside my heart, I knew that I was doing what was right, and refused to respond in frustration, irritation, or discouragement. I simply expressed to God how I felt and found the strength to continue to do his will. I set my heart and mind on accomplishing the tasks: daily evangelism, raising funds, and preparing the revival. I never lost hope or gave up, but persevered in the work. Ask yourself, if God called you to a task would you allow anyone to frustrate you to where you give up on yourself? Or would you determine to complete it, even if you face opposition or discouragement? The rewards only come to those who are faithful and committed to completing the project. I will fulfill my dreams if it meant working alone. There was no stopping me! I was on a road and soaring higher than the storm of strife.

Day 6: I constantly combined prayer with preparation and planning. I trusted God and kept a vigilant watch over what I have been entrusted with, for this was my responsibility as a steward. I prayed and combined prayer with passion, thoughts, preparation, and effort. Accomplishing such a large task is often burdensome, yet I didn't feel like I had a trained disciple that I could assign to oversee this task as I went into prayer. There will always be pressures that foster discouragement; sometimes the task seemed impossible for the delays. My only cure for fatigue and discouragement was to remain focused on God's purpose. I reminded the workers of their task, goal, and God's protection. Often in the natural eyes of a human, it may seem that the project cannot be finished because too many external and internal factors are working against us; but if God is with us who can be against us. (Roman 8:31) Nothing worth having in life ever comes too easily, I was determined to keep my eyes on the prize. Because of the workload, many workers left. I kept my trust in God, "They went out from us, but they did not really belong to us. "For if they had belonged to us, they would have remained with us; but they're going showed that none of them belonged to us." (1 John 2:19 NIV). All I could do was trust God and release those whose heart wasn't truly in it; time to move onto the next steps.

Day 7: I completed all the logistics and administrative work for our first outdoor revival. Finally, that day had come! The outcome of this event was great because most of the people were already at the park and they came over to sit in the seat to hear the word of God. Afterward, I fed the group barbequed chicken. It is very important to nourish people with spiritual food which is the word of God and physical food for strength. We find in Matthew 14:19-21, Jesus feeding five thousand people with only two fish and five loaves of bread. The focus is not just the miracle that took place, but that when God healed people, he showed compassion to feed the sheep. Overall, the event turned out great, but I still wanted to rent a large building to do revivals indoors.

My next project was to work on finding a building to rent, so my church could have an indoor location. I was working hard on funding to make my dreams come true. This was the hardest part. Keep in mind, when I arrived in New York, I was living frugally, with some outstanding loans still active and no consistent income. Still recovering financially, I trusted that God would give me divine hidden mysteries on how I could raise funds for the church and its programs. Working toward having a building was still a work in progress, but no matter what, I would continue to work to fulfill my dream. No slowing down, this is only the beginning.

CHAPTER 15

Life as A Disciple

I'm living life at its best! Now I'm working on three new projects: movie, ministry, and music. I must admit, I can be a workaholic. Honestly, I can't remember the last time I took a vacation, the ministry requires a lot of responsibility. I was so passionate about doing the work of God and getting money to used to dispense to the kingdom, that I became out of balance. It was like having an addiction to exercise, which people define as a "positive addiction," but anything can be harmful if you do too much of it. I was working for the King, but still missing out on the King. Never be too busy doing service you neglect your quiet time with the Lord. For me, although I found joy in using my gifts; I was constantly reaching out to help people, which negatively affected me tremendously. Most of my relationships were one-sided, which isn't healthy. However, I had no one to refill my cup. I've learned in my ministry I faced danger because I was pouring out to people and never receiving. By disconnecting from people and reconnecting with God, my spirit became replenished.

I have experienced major storms in life: One minute; I am a mighty general, and the next day I seem like an ordinary person. I would have a mountaintop experience one day and be in the valley the next day. I was training and raising new leaders to take over my position, however; it was not the fastest process. I should have slowed down and taken time for myself, yet I had such a high demand for calls. Every time someone called me, I would feel obligated to help. I would feel like I would do injustice by ignoring the calls when they really need prayer or a solution to their problems. Is it considered a weakness to always overextend myself to people? If loving people is a weakness, then I don't mind being labeled as the weakest person in the world! Perhaps, I should have set up boundaries and said no, but my compassion and love for people wouldn't allow me. The more I made myself available to help, the more they abuse my love. It seemed as if people only loved me to a certain extent, which was what they could get from me. I didn't know if they were coming to show appreciation to God or coming to receive from God.

For a moment I felt bad, because it was my habit to always make myself available. I was the person who my family or friends could rely on, and loyalty and honesty are the most important for me. Learning to say "no" was a hard lesson for me to get. Sometimes loving people at a distance is the best thing to do. Perhaps, I was too busy taking care of others, and I missed out on my personal time. People were perishing every day, and I just wanted to tell everyone about Jesus. Balance was the key, yet when I told people, "no" they would try to emotionally manipulate me into me feeling like the bad person. They would make it seem as if I was committing a sin by refusing to help those who were in need. However, I must always put what God commands of me first, without being beholden to others' opinions of me. As Paul puts it, "Am I now trying to win the approval of human beings, or of God? Or am I trying to please people? If I were still trying to please people, I would not be a servant of Christ.(Galatians 1:10) Do you spend your life trying to please everybody. Never apologize for honesty and straightforwardness; learn how to set boundaries with other people. Whose approval are you seeking, is it God or others? In all that you do, make sure that you are pleasing the father.

To become a disciple of Jesus Christ or master greatness, it requires great sacrifice. A disciple is someone who believes and follows the teachings of Jesus Christ. The calling of every believer on earth is to evangelize the good news of Jesus. Regardless of your profession on earth, follow on the legacy of the Master during his stay on earth.

For you to become a true disciple, we should employ the following discipline. Endure all persecutions and tribulations as Jesus Christ did. Don't be dismayed that the world might reject you. Jesus says that "if the world hates you, you should know they hated me before you were born. You will be hated by this world because you are not of this world". (John 15:18-19 NIV) Live a Christ-like lifestyle: Be forgiving; learn to forgive others debts and errors, give to people who are less privileged, be kind even to your enemies, be accommodating. Have the heart of a few: Once a while, a disciple gets discontented with his position in Christendom. We, like the disciples in the Bible, over and over might have the desire to get ahead of our fellow believers. However, Christ rebukes this act and instructs us at every point in time. (Matthew 18:1, Matthew 23:11-12, Luke 9:46-43, Luke 22:24,26).

It is necessary to dispose of love for material things, including your own will and love of others as a disciple of Jesus Christ. You will trade all that you are for all that He is. Because we're His treasured possessions; holy and acceptable unto Him. Benefits of being a disciple of Jesus Christ is that although the demands of discipleship are great, he never requires of us anything which he does not give us the strength to do. Our rewards are based more on magnitude than motives. Whatever we lost during following Christ, he rewards us a hundredfold. And above all eternal life. (Mark 10:30)

To become a committed disciple of Christ, one must ask the following questions. Do you want to gain the entire world and lose your life? What will be your gain if you keep eternal life and watch your loved ones lose theirs, knowing you could have done something about it? Would you please your boss, colleagues, friends, and family and displease God? Would you suffer a while on earth or suffer eternal torture in hell? All things said, we have to reflect within ourselves and count the cost of following Christ Jesus.

Jesus said it best in Luke 17:33 NIV, "Whoever tries to keep their life will lose it, and whoever loses their life will preserve it." Those clinging to this life are those seeking to escape physical persecution. Those who are self-seeking and selfish, often live for materialism. They want to work hard and get want, they walk by sight, unseen things are merely ideas and dreams. (not operating out of faith, which is a sin). Individualism people work hard for themselves, instead of for the kingdom of God. Our great reward is to receive the five crowns of life. My advice to new believers: Be faithful, be baptized and patiently endure the present trials and testings in life. Die to self daily and become consecrated through the washing of the word of God. Remember that repentance and forgiveness is a lifestyle for all believers. Faith in Jesus makes us righteous and blameless.

Below are the five crowns we will receive if we run the race without giving up.

CROWN OF LIFE
Qualified: Christian must be faithful, baptized, and patiently endure the present trials and testings in life. Consistently die to self, allow the Holy Spirit to take full control.
Disqualified: Devil can deceive you by false teaching. I advise Christians to read the Bible only!

INCORRUPTIBLE CROWN
Qualified: Be filled with the Holy Spirit, put off the desires of the flesh.
Disqualified: Devil tries to convince Christians and leads them to believe it's okay to sin a little because grace saves you. Satan is a liar, for the Holy Spirit rules flesh.

CROWN OF RIGHTEOUSNESS
Qualified: Believers must be mature in the Word and constantly walk in faith.
Disqualified: Devil tempts believers to give up seeking God's face and praying. Never lose hope in God.

CROWN OF REJOICING

Qualified: Lead people into a deeper relationship with Jesus, helping them gain the Kingdom.

Disqualified: Devil frustrates believer's faith by discouraging them, leading them to despair, and eventually, they give up on faith. Never leave the church. Stay connected to your pastor and fellowship of your community.

CROWN OF GLORY

Qualified: Meditate on the Scriptures. Nourish the flock of God with the deeper truths from God's Word.

Disqualified: Devil steals crown by saying it's reserved for the pastor. Salvation is for everyone.

Choose life in Jesus Christ, not death. "We are more than conquerors through him who loved us." (Romans 8:37 NIV) We shall overcome the cross, even to the point of death, we shall rule with Jesus Christ for 1,000 years. Hallelujah! Make your commitment today to follow Jesus forever.

CHAPTER 16

Holy Land Experience

Come with me to the Holy Land, to walk in Jesus's footsteps, in the very places he traveled 2000 years ago. Having relatives living in Israel gave me the perfect opportunity to see that part of the world. where I wanted to plant ministry and work with business investors.

When I finally arrived in Israel, I had to go through the security check which took longer than I thought, which gave me look around at all the fascinating. After several hours of waiting, I was finally able to go in. Israel reminded me of New York City because it was so diverse. Yet, it felt very safe. Then, I notice that several off-duty soldiers walked around with weapons; they were loaded with m16s at the mall, parks, and even the beach. I found that strange as I begin to drive around in my car rental. Also, I notice that the police didn't give tickets to the electric bikes on the highways; it was lawful for them to drive in the street along with cars and trucks. There was so much for me to get used to living in this new place; I had to figure out transportation, parking, controlling my expenses, without getting too involved. Parking was just like New York City, it was expensive and nearly impossible to find a lot available. Fortuitously, I had a small car so I could easily parallel park, and use meter parking on the street. Struggling with another language, I ran into difficulties with some people, but most people knew English, and I was able to get along with my knowledge of the Hebrew language.

As I left the bank to grab money for my travels, I decided to drive to McDonald's in Israel. The McDonald's salad menu was different from the United States, but the quality of chicken salad tastes fresher. I notice that the food was very expensive in Israel. In fact, it cost more than public transportation. Due to the complications of finding parking, I drop my car off to the airport and decided to take public transportation. This was overall better because I could save money on parking and traffic, and public transportation was faster.

I took the train from Tel Aviv to Nazareth, then onto the town where my family members lived. When I arrived, I greeted everyone with a holy kiss and hug; and my family surprised me with a nice meal. Afterward, we drove to the Dead sea. It was great, so full of salt that I was able to float easily-- you could practically lie on top of it! The salt water was the best for the skin, and after swimming in that rich water, my skin had a nice glow. The Dead Sea is known for its healing properties and is said to work on all manner of skin problems, sore muscles, and to stimulate blood circulation. This place was just beautiful and I had fun taking pictures.

I intended to stay with my family for the whole week, but my plans were interrupted when, a few days later, I received a call from my brother in the Lord to ask me to preach at the church in Tel-Aviv. I was so torn; I had promised my family I would stay, but when my ministry calls, I feel that it's my duty to answer. My short mini family vacation was over; it was time for me to win souls for the Kingdom of God.

The next day, I left to join my church family to preach at a powerful 3-day Revival in Tel-Aviv. The leader here took such good care of me; he made me feel so safe and comfortable. He even sent his assistants to check to see if I needed anything. It was a blessing to be connected with somebody who was passionate about winning souls for the kingdom like I was, who understood me, and shared similar goals.

After the prophetic revival, we begin to discuss program and strategies on how we can raise money to fund the ministry. That very day, we decided to set up spiritual tours. It was so wonderful to be in partnership to create our spiritual tours, which were typically three days in duration. We rented four buses, preaching and singing hymns on the bus. We played bible study games, watched bible-based movies, and had give-aways. The spirit was one of having fun; we didn't want learning about Jesus to feel like drudgery.

We started at the Sea of Galilee, where we said morning intercession prayer with the participants, to set the tone of the day. It was important to start the tour at this holy site, as Jesus' earthly ministry centered around the Sea and he performed the majority of his miracles in this area. Ready to board the bus again, we drove about 40 minutes to the Church of the Nativity in Bethlehem, where Jesus Christ was born. Each person had the opportunity to kneel the spot where the manger would be for personal prayer. Of course, like every tourist spot, you have to exit through the gift shop and we bought souvenirs.

The River Jordan was our next stop, which was the very place where John the Baptist baptized Jesus. All of the leaders and I baptized the people on the tour. Such a moving experience, I was honored to be a part of the momentous event. With everybody's clothing still wet, we had the perfect time for meditation class, so we went onto the Mount of Olives, the place where Jesus ascended to heaven. After that, we went to the Church of the Holy Sepulchre, where the tomb where Jesus was originally buried from and a most sacred place and we anointed our prayer shawls.

The next day, we visited the Via Dolorosa, the pathway of the passion of the cross, where I took an opportunity to preach to my group from the tour. Afterward, we went to the Garden of Gethsemane, where Jesus prepared for his crucifixion and was betrayed. Then, we needed a break and headed to Lions Gate and Damascus Gate for shopping and lunch, which is a big tourist attraction. As our group were all God's models, we set up a photo-shoot at the famous Western Wall. As evening came, we went to the Tombs of the Prophets, which was so dark that we needed candles to see. The setting was perfect for my Bible lecture.

As another morning came, and we had our first prayer time at Prophet Elijah Cave and Mountain, where there was a library to study biblical history and took the time to teach about Elijah defeating the Baals. After that, we went to Masada National Park, to take in the natural beauty of the area. We then went to the Negev Desert, which reminded me of the US Grand Canyon in Arizona and we all enjoyed watching the sun go down. Nearby was Abraham's well, where there are many exhibits of old testament scenes and we sat in that beauty reflecting on Abraham and the history of Israel. While in the desert, we had great fun riding camels. After the heat of the desert, we all needed to cool of and let off some steam at Java Beach in Tel Aviv. We enjoyed some of the best food, shopping, and photo ops in the world. Lastly, we ended the evening in quiet meditation at Zachariah Cave also known as Solomon's Quarries.

The time came for me to be alone and reconnect with nature. I treated myself to a mini vacation on a private boat tour to Egypt and Jordan. I hired a professional diver, and I went swimming and scuba diving. I jumped off the boat into the Red Sea and begin to swim with the instructor. My private vacation was over, and I headed back to work. Focusing on working a full-time ministry and evangelizing the good news, I stayed in Israel for a couple of months. Since I decided to stay there a little longer, I had to find an apartment to stay in.

I went out by myself to various areas, without the church family to personally reach out to people, spreading the good news of the gospel of Jesus Christ. At a coffee shop, I met a man who seemed to resist my teachings and looked depressed. Finally, I got him to open up. He asked me, "Why do bad things happen to good people, if there is a God, then why is there still suffering?" It reminded me of the scripture, "Neither this man nor his parents sinned," said Jesus, "but this happened so that the works of God might be displayed in him." (John 9:3 NIV) I explained to him that Christ used this man's suffering to teach about faith and to glorify God. I told him: "We live in a fallen world where good behavior is not always rewarded and bad behavior not always punished. Therefore, innocent people sometimes suffer. If God took suffering away whenever we asked, we would follow him for comfort and convenience, not out of love and devotion. Regardless of the reason for suffering, Jesus has the power to help people deal with it. Ask God to give you the supernatural strength for the trial and a clearer perspective on what is happening." Immediately I saw that this was an opportunity to share my testimony on how I overcame my trials with the power of Jesus Christ and encouraged him to do the same. We discussed biblical teachings, but over our long conversation, I won him over and he was open to hear more about the bible. God works in mysterious ways, and I could see that all that I had been through was not in vain.

As Christians, we should follow the same example: spending time with the poor, rich, bad, good. Do you find yourself neglecting people based on their reputation? If so, know that they are the ones who need you the most- model the Father's love in you and through you. By showing them Christ's love, they will be drawn to know the God you serve. Then they will follow you as you follow Christ Jesus.

I was thankful that God was using me in a mighty way. No matter where I travel to preach the Word of God, Israel will always be special to me. I will continue to work and build disciples for the Kingdom, as I continue to expand the ministry. I was feeling better than ever before and this was only the beginning.

One thing I learned in Israel is that they don't compromise on the Sabbath Shalom day; from Friday afternoon to Saturday everything is shut down in Israel. I mean, throughout the whole country, all non-essential services stop on the Sabbath. Also, on Sabbath shalom day, I noticed that it was completely quiet in the streets. I admired their practice and would encourage anybody to honor the Sabbath, whether it be on a Saturday or Sunday, as for Christians. From Exodus 20:8-9 NIV, "Remember the Sabbath day by keeping it holy. Six days you shall labor and do all your work." You don't have to wait for the stores to be closed to take time for yourself and appreciate what the Lord has done for you and given to you.

I ended my last day visiting a live concert and a carnival at a park with Hebrew artists, Broadway shows, and comedy acts. Later that evening, I visited my church family. I mentioned a couple of days before that I would be leaving. These people certainly demonstrated God's love; they over-extended their welcoming hospitality toward me. I blessed the congregation and my church family prayed for God to give me traveling mercy for my long flight back to the United States.

God sent me to many places throughout the world. Who knows what's next for me? Wherever I'm led, I know I am under the Watchful Eyes of God.

ABOUT THE AUTHOR

Nadia Awwad, a former model and actress, studied business marking at the University of Houston Texas. Soon after, she appeared in several television commercials, one for PBS and one promoting Houston Community College, where she then became the school's branding model for their magazines and marketing materials. Nadia attracted attention as a model and actress worldwide, and she was later featured as a cover model for JMZ Magazine, and began more commercials starting with Doritos. As the words of others glorified her physical image in print and video, her fame rose fast and her fortune increased. She went from the worlds model to God's model. Before moving into the ministry, Nadia became a top salesperson for Johnson & Johnson pharmaceuticals, consistently exceeding sales quotas and goals and managing major hospital accounts. Although highly successful in sales, Nadia was called to the ministry, found a mentor, devoted herself to intense training, and planted churches in Texas and Nigeria. She is devoted to operate full time in her prophetic and spiritual gifts: healing, prophecy, and preaching the undiluted word of God. Her dedication is to give people the proper care, compassion, and support for overcoming any of life's trials. The goal is to help people get healed and become their best version.

CPSIA information can be obtained
at www.ICGtesting.com
Printed in the USA
BVHW031031200619
551533BV00006B/135/P